Oh!
Christmas
Trees

Compiled by Barbara Weiland

That Patchwork Place®

Contributors

Christal Carter   Mimi Dietrich
Kathy Gist and Karol Hervey
Lynette Jensen   Joan Gaestel Macfarlane
Debbie Mumm   Susie Robbins
Sue Thom   Barbara Tourtillotte
Barbara Weiland

Acknowledgments

A special thank you to Susan I. Jones, Nancy J. Martin, Marion Shelton, and Barbara Weiland, who graciously allowed us to take over their homes and set up Christmas trees for the photography in this book. Christmas came early!

Credits

Editor-in-Chief .... Barbara Weiland
Technical Editor .... Barbara Weiland
Managing Editor .... Greg Sharp
Copy Editor .... Liz McGehee
Proofreader .... Tina Cook
Text and Cover Design ....Kay Green
Production .... Dani Ritchardson
Typesetting .... Shean Bemis
Illustration and Graphics .... Laurel Strand
Stephanie Benson
Photography .... Brent Kane
Photo Stylist .... Christal Carter
Photo Stylist Assistants .... Susan I. Jones
Marion Shelton

Oh! Christmas Trees©
©1994 by That Patchwork Place, Inc.,
PO Box 118
Bothell, WA 98041-0118
USA

Printed in Canada
99 98 97 96 95 94   6 5 4 3 2 1

Oh! Christmas trees / edited by Barbara Weiland.
     p. cm.
  ISBN 1-56477-062-1 :
  1. Patchwork—Patterns. 2. Trees in art. 3. Christmas trees.
4. Christmas decorations. I. Weiland, Barbara. II. That Patchwork
Place, Inc.
TT835.039 1994
745.594'12—dc20   94-18423
                                                   CIP

That Patchwork Place Mission Statement

We are dedicated to providing quality products that encourage creativity and promote self-esteem in our customers and our employees.

We strive to make a difference in the lives we touch.

That Patchwork Place is an employee-owned, financially secure company.

Contents

Introduction

Oh! Christmas Trees celebrates the joy of the Christmas season and the creative spirit in all of us. The idea for this book evolved out of an impromptu brainstorming discussion with my assistant, Marion Shelton. We both love stitching and crafting and we both love Christmas, so when Marion made note of an article about a quilt guild that sold raffle tickets for a handmade designer Christmas tree to benefit a local charity, our collective creative wheels started spinning. "Why not invite quilt and craft designers to submit ideas for designer Christmas trees for a new book?" we said. So we did, and this book is the result!

On the following pages, you will find fully illustrated directions and patterns for re-creating ten unique Christmas trees. You're sure to find one—or several—that will appeal to your interests and fit into your Christmas decorating scheme. Each tree features a variety of projects—ornaments, Christmas stockings, tree skirts, quilted wall hangings, wreaths, and table runners. You need only a little imagination and some basic stitching and crafting skills to create your own version of your favorite tree. Feel free to play with the color schemes, changing them to suit your tastes.

You could easily change the Victorian Elegance tree into a country look by using less opulent fabrics in country colors, for example. And Baltimore Nosegays don't have to be red like those in this book. Make these pretty ribbon roses in any color that suits your fancy and your decorating scheme. Use them for package decorations or table favors for a holiday luncheon if you prefer. Many of the trees feature co-ordinating Christmas stockings and each one is a little different. If you prefer the shape of one of the stockings with a tree other than the one you are doing, feel free to make substitutions.

The trees in this book require materials easily located at fabric, craft, and floral shops. For most projects, you will need a sewing machine in good working order, an iron, and some basic sewing supplies. For some of the projects, you will also need a glue gun and plenty of glue. The quilted projects scattered throughout this book are simple to sew, with step-by-step directions that beginners will find easy to follow.

You may not wish to re-create an entire tree. In that case, enjoy making the individual projects to add to your growing collection of Christmas decorations. Many would make wonderful gifts for those who love Christmas as much as you do. And several of the quilts are suitable for use throughout the year, not just for Christmas.

The directions with each tree include a Trim-the-Tree Shopping List, so you will know what you need to buy to re-create the trees as they appear in the color photographs at the beginning of each chapter. You may already have some of the pictured embellishments and you may decide to use additional items to personalize your tree.

When I sat down to write this introduction, the words of Kathy Gist and Karol Hervey rang in my ears because they had expressed so eloquently what this book is all about.

"Christmas is more than a time of year; it is a feeling that touches our hearts as no other holiday does. No matter how hectic and busy our lives, somehow we find time to shop, cook, send cards, entertain, and decorate our homes. One family may use religious symbols to express a deep faith; another may decorate with the toys, bright colors, and handmade ornaments that capture a child's magical view of Christmas. The ideal Christmas may be a winter wonderland, a dance with the Sugarplum Fairy, or a rustic retreat with a crackling fire and a hand-hewn tree. However we celebrate it, Christmas allows us to express our feelings openly."

Christmas is also a time to express the joy we find in exercising our creative abilities in a way that we can visibly share with those dear to us. I hope that you will find plenty of inspiration in this book to fill happy moments for years to come, stitching and crafting the Christmas tree(s) of your dreams to enjoy with family and friends.

Barbara Weiland

Barbara Weiland
Editor

Victorian Elegance

by Barbara Weiland

This stately tree is lavishly decorated to evoke Victorian Christmas memories. Use elegant fabrics, such as velveteen, moiré faille, and tapestry with gold lamé embellishments to re-create this sumptuous look.

▲ *Make a host of heavenly angels in pink moiré with sparkle-organza wings and Spanish moss hair. Mini stockings in velveteen, gold lamé, and tapestry are quick to stitch, using ready-made trimmings.*

A luxurious sweep of tapestry, moiré faille, and velveteen make a splendid tree skirt, accented with gold lamé piping and elegant tassels. ▼

▲ *Golden pouches of ribbon are folded and embellished to hide tiny treasures or hold fragrant potpourri. These are special enough to be small gifts by themselves.*

▲ *Posh Christmas stockings hung in anticipation of St. Nicholas' visit are the perfect addition to the mantel.*

Charming beribboned fans echo the Victorian style amid dozens of sparkling organza snowflakes. ▶

◀ *This divine angel is equally at home on the top of the tree or standing regally on the mantel. Embellish a brass horn with silk poinsettias and greens to herald the season and hang as a wreath above the fireplace or on your front door.*

*L*ush colors and luxurious fabrics of bygone eras have always held a special fascination for me. I especially cherish vintage fabrics and fashions from the Victorian era, finding it difficult to cut into those in my collection, even when not in pristine condition. My love of Victoriana was the inspiration for this Christmas tree. To evoke a feeling of Victorian elegance in our obviously contemporary home, I combined cranberry velveteen, pink moiré faille, gold tissue lamé, and patchwork tapestry shot with gold, then accented them with a lavish assortment of ribbons and trim to fashion an opulent tree skirt and matching stockings. The rich array of handmade ornaments requires minimal sewing skills. Assorted glass ornaments, cranberry bead garlands, candles in brass clips, lots of white lights, and large silk poinsettias in cranberry and pink add the finishing touches to this memorable ten-foot tree that sweeps to the top of the cathedral ceiling in our living room.

The fireplace and mantel and the stair railings that lead up to the living room were decorated with artificial swags dressed in pink poinsettias. Candles and lights sparkle amidst the greenery on the mantel, and stately reindeer stand guard in this beautiful Christmas setting.

Barbara Weiland

Barbara Weiland has had an ongoing love affair with fabric and needlecrafts since her great-grandmother taught her to make doll clothes when she was only eight. That love affair grew into a career in the home sewing and publishing fields. Currently, Barbara is the editor-in-chief at That Patchwork Place, where she is responsible for planning what the company will publish and then working with authors and editors to create finished books for readers.

Barbara has written several books, including a cookbook, one on wardrobe planning, and others on various sewing topics. In her spare time, when she is not doing free-lance writing for *Sew News* or taking voice lessons, she sews and crafts—clothing, gifts, home-decorating items, and quilts. Barbara shares her busy life in Redmond, Washington, with her husband, Lou Kiersky.

Trim-the-Tree Shopping List

✔ Pink, cranberry, and clear iridescent glass balls in assorted sizes

✔ Clear glass balls, stuffed with iridescent tinsel*

✔ Clusters of large pink and burgundy silk poinsettias**

✔ Brass candle clips and white candles

✔ White mini lights

✔ Artificial cranberry garlands (wooden and gold beads)

✔ Gold foil wrapping paper

✔ 2"-wide pink velvet wire-edged ribbon for packages

✔ Burgundy and gold wire-edged ribbon for packages

✔ Artificial pine garlands for mantel and stairway

✔ Pink silk-poinsettia garlands for mantel and stairway (or individual silk poinsettias removed from bunches of poinsettias)

✔ Pink wire-edged taffeta ribbon bow for mantel

✔ Candles and candleholders for mantel

*Remove the crown from clear glass balls and use a pencil or a chopstick to coax a handful of tinsel inside. Replace the crown.

**Use wire cutters to cut stems from ready-made bouquets, then tuck flowers in the branches close to the tree trunk to add color to areas that don't have ornaments.

Heavenly Angel Ornament

Finished Size: 5" x 5½"

These sweet little angels guard the tree by day and night and require minimal machine and hand sewing. Crystalline wings made by fusing layers of sparkle organza together keep them ever in flight.

Materials for 1 ornament

4" x 8" rectangle of pink moiré for body
Scrap of Ultrasuede® or felt in flesh tone for head
4" x 21" piece of white polyester sparkle organza for wings
4" x 10½" piece of paper-backed fusible web, such as Wonder-Under
6"-long piece of ⅛"-wide ribbon for hanging loop
4"-diameter lace doily for collar
Seam sealant, such as Fray Check™ (optional)
1 tiny burgundy satin rose
Spanish moss for hair
Gold wire or gold star garland for halo
Fiberfill for stuffing
Glue gun and glue

Assembly

Use patterns on page 26 and the wing pattern on pullout pattern sheet #1. Refer to photo on page 7.

1. Cut 2 body pieces from the pink moiré and 2 head pieces from the Ultrasuede.
2. With right sides facing, stitch the body pieces together, leaving an opening for turning as marked. Turn right side out and press, turning under the seam allowance at the opening edges.

Leave open.

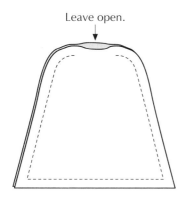

3. *With wrong sides together,* stitch the face pieces a scant ⅛" from the raw edge. Set aside.
4. Cut the organza into 2 pieces, each 4" x 10½". Following manufacturer's instructions, apply fusible web to 1 piece of organza. Remove the backing paper and fuse to the remaining piece of organza. Cut 2 wings from the resulting piece.
5. Layer the wings and make a small pinch pleat in the center. Pin. Fold the 6" length of ribbon in half to make a loop and pin to wing at pleat. Machine stitch through all layers.

Stitch scant ⅛" from raw edges.

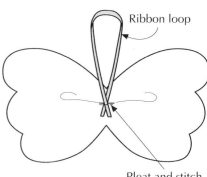

Ribbon loop

Pleat and stitch.

6. Stuff the angel body and head firmly with fiberfill. Tuck the head into the opening in the body and whipstitch in place.
7. Cut a small hole in the center of doily if it does not have a hole already. If an existing hole is too small, make it just large enough to fit snugly over the head. If desired, treat the cut edges with a seam sealant.
8. Gently tug the doily over the angel's head. Sew or glue a satin rose (and a small bow if desired) in the center. Arrange Spanish moss for the hair and glue in place using the glue gun. Make a halo from a 5½" length of gold wire or star garland and glue to the back of the head.
9. Glue wings in place on the back of the angel, placing the pinch pleat just below the neck, with the ribbon ends against the angel.

Whipst body to

Add ha

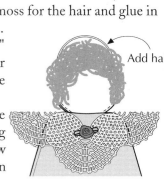

Spun Sugar Balls

Finished Size: 3" diameter

The sugarplum fairies left a gilded edge on these frothy balls, lavished with ribbons and beautiful sugar-crusted berries. They are deceivingly simple to make, but you will need a serger to finish the edges of the pink squares that cover the Styrofoam™ balls. If you don't own a serger, spend a day with a friend who does and leave a batch of these ornaments behind as a "thank you." If that's not possible, you may pink the edges instead.

Materials for 1 ornament

Gold metallic machine embroidery thread
12" square of pink polyester sparkle organza
3"-diameter Styrofoam ball
12"-long pink chenille stem (pipe cleaner)
12"-long piece *each* of ⅛"-wide gold, light green, and
    burgundy ribbons
1 stem of leaves and berries (pink and green)*
Small rubber band
Fine knitting needle

*I bought preassembled stems in the floral department, then disassembled them and made bunches that included 5 leaves in assorted sizes, a cluster or two of berries, and a corkscrew wire.

Assembly

1. Thread your serger with pink thread in the needle and gold metallic machine embroidery thread in the loopers and adjust for a closely spaced, wide stitch. Test on fabric scraps.
2. Serge the edges of the sparkle organza square.

3. Use a fine knitting needle to poke a hole through the center of the Styrofoam ball.
4. Fold the chenille stem in half and push through the hole, so 2" of wire extends at the bottom of the ball. Turn up ¼" at each end of the wire that extends and push back into the bottom of the ball. Pull on the loop at the top of the ball to tighten.
5. Center the ball in the fabric square and draw up the fabric around the loop. Secure with a rubber band.
6. Wrap the leaf/berry stem around the neck of the ornament securely.
7. Holding the ornament between your knees to steady it, wrap the ribbons around the neck to cover the stem and tie securely in a square knot. Cut ribbon ends the desired length at an angle. Arrange the leaves and berries as desired to cover the ribbon knot.

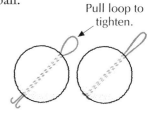

Pull loop to tighten.

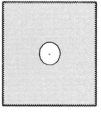

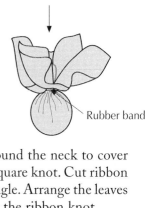

Rubber band

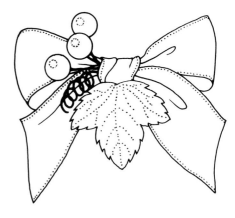

Gilded Wreaths

Finished Size: 4" diameter, plus bow

Tiny angels perch in these glitter-splashed wreaths trimmed with ribbon and bright berries.

Materials for 1 ornament

1 woven vine wreath (4" diameter)
1 miniature ceramic or plastic angel figurine*
20"-long piece of gold wire-edged ribbon
1 berry cluster (3 berries, 1 leaf, and a spiral)**
12"- to 16"-long piece of ⅛"- or ³⁄₁₆"-wide double-faced burgundy satin ribbon
Glue gun and glue
Gold spray paint
Gold glitter spray paint

*You may substitute other seasonal miniatures.
**Buy a spray of berries and leaves and take apart. Reassemble into clusters, using 3 berries of different sizes if possible. If your berry spray does not have spirals, you can make them by winding a length of paper-covered florist wire around a pencil. Remove pencil and spray the spiral with gold paint.

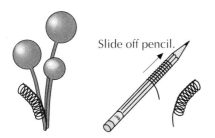

Slide off pencil.

Assembly

1. Glue the figurine to the wreath and allow to cool.
2. Spray paint the wreath and figurine with the gold paint and then the glitter paint, allowing to dry between each coat.
3. Make a bow out of the gold ribbon and cut the ends at an angle.
4. Wrap the stems of the berries, leaf, and spiral together and tuck the end through the top of the knot in the bow. Then wind the wire to the back of the bow and cut off excess wire.

5. Glue completed bow with berries to the wreath just below the figurine and arrange berries and leaf.
6. Thread satin ribbon under a vine at the top of the wreath and tie in a square knot. Tie ends together in an overhand knot and cut off excess at an angle.

Beribboned Fans

Finished Size: 4" x 8"

Victorian women were never without their fans. Roses, made from wire-edged ribbon, and ribbon streamers are glued to the fused, folded, and stitched fan shapes. Perch these pretty fans on tree branches—no hangers required.

Materials for 4 fans

¼ yd. of 54"-wide pink or burgundy moiré faille*
⅜ yd. of 18"-wide paper-backed fusible web, such as Wonder-Under
1½ yds. of 1"-wide wire-edged gold lamé ribbon for roses
3 yds. of ⅛"-wide gold ribbon or trim
3 yds. of ⅛"-wide light green ribbon
1½ yds. of ⅛"-wide pink ribbon
1½ yds. of ⅛"-wide burgundy ribbon

*Make sure fabric piece is 9" x 54" when straightened. Buy ⅜ yd. to be safe.

Assembly

1. Cut 3 strips of fusible web, each 4½" x 18".
2. Following manufacturer's instructions, apply fusible web to the wrong side of the 9" x 54" moiré strip. Allow to cool.
3. Fold the moiré strip in half lengthwise, wrong sides together, and fuse the 2 layers together.

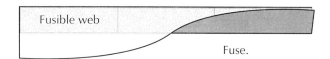
Fusible web · Fuse.

4. Cut the strip into 4 equal lengths.
5. Zigzag or closely serge the raw edge of each strip to finish.

Fold · Serge or zigzag raw edges.

6. Accordion fold each strip in ½"-wide pleats, making sure that raw edges face the same direction when folding is completed. Use your finger to firmly crease each

fold. To help set the pleats, anchor the folded strip to the ironing board with a pin at each end and press. Allow to cool.

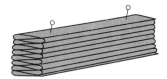

Anchor pleats with pins.

7. Cut the wire-edged ribbon into 4 equal lengths.

8. Draw up the wire on one edge for ½" or so to begin the gathering. Turn the wire back onto the ribbon; turn the ribbon edge down at a 45° angle, then back onto itself; secure with a few stitches. Leave the needle and thread attached.

Draw up ½" of wire.   Turn wire back onto ribbon.

Turn ribbon end under at 45° angle.

9. Draw up the wire at the other end of the ribbon to gather into a rose shape and hand stitch the layers together on the underside. Turn under the remaining raw edge and hand stitch to finish.

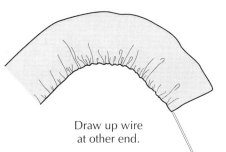 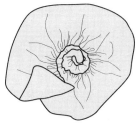

Draw up wire at other end.

10. Cut the ⅛"-wide ribbon into 13" lengths. For each fan, make a bundle of ribbons, using 2 gold, 2 green, and 1 each of the pink and burgundy. Tie in an overhand knot, centering the knot along the length.

Center knot

11. Glue the knot of each ribbon bundle to the back of a rose. Allow to cool.

12. Thread a sturdy needle with doubled thread and thread the bottom edge of the fan pleats together as shown. Draw up the thread and securely whipstitch the bottom edges of the 2 outermost pleats together as shown.

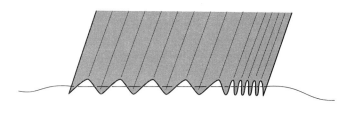

Fan back

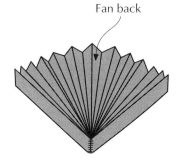

Stitch edges together.

13. Glue a rose with ribbons to the bottom of each fan.

14

Poinsettia Stars

Finished Size: Approximately 6½" across

This tree would not be complete without a sprinkling of glittering stars. They require gold lamé knit, fusible web, and purchased silk poinsettias.

Materials for 3 stars

¼ yd. of 54"-wide tricot-backed gold lamé*
½ yd. of 18"-wide paper-backed fusible web, such as Wonder-Under
18"-long piece of gold cord
3 gold poinsettias (plastic or silk). Those shown were cut from a stem of poinsettias purchased at a craft store.
Press cloth
Glue gun and glue

*Do not try this with tissue lamé. It doesn't work. If tricot-backed lamé is not available, look for other gold fabrics and test by fusing 2 layers and making a star as directed below.

Assembly

Use the pattern on page 27.

1. Cut a gold lamé strip 9" x 54". Cut in half to make 2 pieces, each 9" x 27".
2. Cut 1 strip of paper-backed fusible web, 9" x 18", and 1 piece 9" x 9".
3. Following the manufacturer's instructions, apply the strips of fusible web to the wrong side of the 9" x 27" lamé piece. Allow to cool.

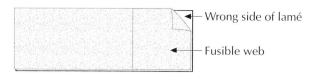
— Wrong side of lamé
— Fusible web

4. Remove the backing paper and fuse to the wrong side of the remaining strip of lamé. *Use a press cloth to protect the lamé surface* and do not press any longer than necessary to achieve a secure fuse. *Be careful not to touch the iron to the surface of the lamé.*

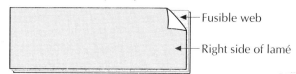
— Fusible web
— Right side of lamé

5. Cut 3 star pieces from the fused lamé strip, cutting out the hole in the center of each one.
6. Thread a sturdy needle with double, waxed thread and do a running stitch ⅛" from the edge of the inner hole. Pull up to gather and take a few backstitches to secure.
7. Cut the gold cord into 3 equal lengths.
8. Make the cord into a loop and glue to the back of the star, adding a poinsettia in the center of the star on the front. If the flower is attached to a stem, poke the stem through the center of the star, cut the stem even with the star, and apply glue to the stem and gathered edges of the star.

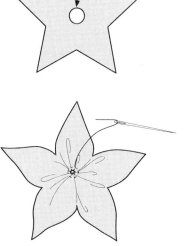
Cut out.

Golden Ribbon Pocket

Finished Size: 2" x 3", plus hanger

Pretty little pockets are the perfect finishing touch at branch ends. A bit of lace plus ribbons and flowers embellish these golden trinkets made from wire-edged ribbon. Use them to embellish packages if you like, or consider filling them with potpourri or a small gift.

Materials for 1 pocket

7"-long piece of 2"-wide gold wire-edged ribbon
6"-long piece of ⅛"-wide burgundy ribbon for hanger
1 small lace medallion, approximately 1½" wide*
6 pieces of ⅛" x 10" double-faced satin ribbon in assorted colors: mint green, dark green, pink, and burgundy
3 small satin roses (pink, burgundy, and white) or a gold silk poinsettia (2" to 2½" in diameter) with a small burgundy satin rose glued to the center, or a berry-and-leaf cluster
Glue gun and glue
Polyester fiberfill
Chopstick

*You can buy white lace by the yard with the correct-size motifs and cut them from the lace. This is much less expensive than buying individual lace pieces.

Assembly

1. At each end of the gold wire-edged ribbon, turn under ¼" and then an additional ¼", finger-pressing each fold. The wire in the edges of the ribbon will hold this "hem" in place so stitching is unnecessary.

Turn ¼" *twice* at each end of ribbon.

2. Turn up one end of the ribbon to a depth of 2½" and crease to form the pocket.

3. Tuck one end of the 6" length of burgundy ribbon into the folded edge at the top of the pocket. Using a zipper foot, stitch next to the wire, catching the ribbon in the stitching. Repeat with the other end of the ribbon on the other side of the pocket.

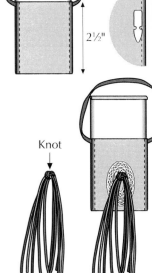
2½"

4. Using the glue gun sparingly, glue the lace to the pocket.

5. With all 6 ribbons in a bundle, tie a knot that is centered along the length. Glue ribbon to lace.

6. Arrange 3 ribbon roses, a gold silk poinsettia with a burgundy rose, or a berry-and-leaf cluster on the pocket to cover the ribbon knot. Glue in place. Trim ribbon ends at an angle to a pleasing length.

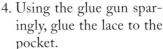
Knot

Ribbon bundle

7. Gently stuff the pocket with fiberfill, using the point of a chopstick to tuck it into the corners.

8. Turn the top edge of the ribbon down over the top edge of the pocket to finish.

Mini Stocking

Finished Size: 6" x 8"

There's probably a baby or two on your Christmas list for whom these ornaments would make a perfect stocking for their first Christmas. Consider filling these with tiny treasures to hang on the tree, then give as gifts or party favors to holiday visitors—if you can part with them, that is!

Materials for 1 stocking

6¼" x 9¼" piece of cranberry velveteen for the back of stocking*

6¼" x 9¼" piece of tapestry for front of stocking

Narrow gold rickrack or trim

5" x 8½" piece of pink moiré for cuff

8½"-long piece of ½"-wide gold ribbon

1 burgundy satin rose

5 lengths of ⅛"-wide ribbon, each 18" long, in burgundy, gold, pink, light green, and medium green

*If you prefer, make some stockings with velveteen on both front and back.

Assembly

Use pattern on pullout pattern sheet #1.
Refer to photo on page 7.

1. Cut 1 stocking from velveteen and 1 from tapestry, making sure to cut so you have a front (tapestry) and a back (velveteen).
2. Pin rickrack or trim in place on the stocking front at heel and toe. Stitch in place.

3. With right sides together, stitch the stocking pieces ¼" from the raw edges. Clip the curves. Trim the seam in the curved heel and toe areas to ³⁄₁₆". Zigzag the seam allowances together.

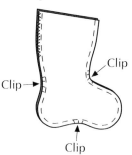

4. Turn the stocking right side out and press carefully.
5. Pin the gold ribbon to the right side of the pink moiré strip with the top edge of the ribbon 1⅛" from the top edge of the strip. Stitch in place.

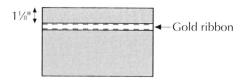

6. With right sides together, stitch the short ends of the cuff ¼" from the raw edge. Press the seam open. Turn right side out. Fold the cuff in half, wrong sides together.

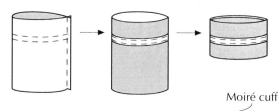

7. Pin the cuff to the top edge of the stocking, *with the gold ribbon against the wrong side of the stocking.* Stitch ¼" from the raw edge.
8. Turn the cuff to the outside and press. Sew or glue the satin rose to the gold ribbon.
9. Gather all 5 ribbons together and fold in half. Tie an overhand knot to form a loop approximately 2" long.
10. Sew loop securely to the top edge of the cuff at the left side.

Sparkle Snowflakes

Finished Size: 3" diameter

If you made paper snowflakes as a child, you'll find these 3-D snowflakes easy to make. A little fusing, pinking, and snipping, and you'll have dozens done in no time!

Materials for 2 snowflakes

4" x 32" strip of white polyester sparkle organza
4" x 16" strip of paper-backed fusible web, such as
    Wonder-Under
24"-long piece of narrow ribbon for loop
White fabric glue
Paper clips
Pinking shears
Small, sharp scissors

Assembly

1. Cut the strip of organza into 2 pieces, each 4" x 16".
2. Following manufacturer's instructions, apply fusible web to 1 piece of organza. Allow to cool. Remove paper and fuse to the remaining piece of organza.
3. Cut the resulting strip in half crosswise so you have 2 pieces, each 4" x 8".
4. Pink the long edges of each strip.

5. Accordion-fold each rectangle, short end to short end, in ½" pleats, firmly creasing each fold with your fingers. Cut out a small wedge of fabric at the center on each long side as shown.

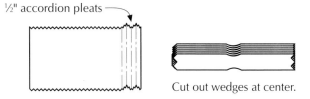

½" accordion pleats

Cut out wedges at center.

6. Cut wedges on each side of the center wedge. Due to the thickness and stiffness of the fabric, you may need to cut each separately. It's OK if the wedges are not exactly the same size and shape.

7. Cut the ribbon into 2 equal lengths. Center a ribbon on each folded, notched rectangle and machine stitch through all layers. Glue the ribbon to the fabric and allow to dry.

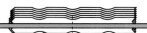

Glue ribbon in place.

8. Run a thin line of glue down the center of the ribbon. Bring the unconnected pleats together and hold in place with a few paper clips. Allow to dry. Glue and clip the remaining 2 unconnected pleats together at the bottom of the snowflake. Remove the paper clips when glue is dry.

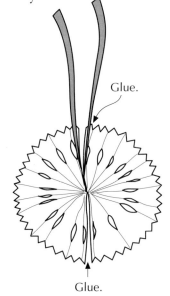

Glue.

Glue.

9. Tie the ends of the ribbon in an overhand knot to complete the hanging loop.

Tapestry Tree Skirt

Finished Size: 60" diameter

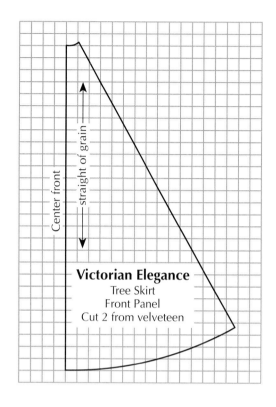

Victorian Elegance
Tree Skirt
Front Panel
Cut 2 from velveteen

Alternating panels of tapestry and velveteen are set off with shirred puffing strips of moiré and purchased gold piping in this elegant skirt. If piping is not readily available, make your own by wrapping strips of gold tissue lamé around cording available in the home-decorating department of many fabric stores.

Materials

1½ yds. pattern tracing cloth or tissue paper
1½ yds. of 54"-wide tapestry for skirt panels
1½ yds. of 54"-wide cranberry velveteen or velvet for skirt panels
1¾ yds. of 54"-wide pink moiré faille for puffing strips and ties (There will be some leftover fabric to use for other ornaments if desired.)
9 yds. of gold lamé piping
7 yds. of ½"-wide flexible gold trim
2 large gold drapery cord tassels for ties

Cutting

1. Following the graph at right, draft the skirt pattern pieces and cut them from pattern tracing cloth or tissue paper.
2. From the tapestry, cut 3 full skirt panels.
3. From the velveteen, cut 2 full skirt panels and 2 front panels, making sure to follow the nap and cutting a left and right front.
4. From the moiré faille, cut 6 strips, each 3¾" wide, cutting along the length of the fabric (parallel to the selvages). From the remaining fabric, cut enough 3"-wide true-bias strips to make a piece 60" long.

Victorian Elegance
Tree Skirt
Full Panel
Cut 3 from tapestry
Cut 2 from velveteen

1 square = 1"

Assembly

Refer to photo on page 7.

Note: All seam allowances are ½" wide.

1. Fold each full skirt panel in half along each long edge and mark the center fold with a ⅛"-deep snip. Do the same with each front panel, but do not snip-mark the center front edges. Repeat with each moiré strip, snip-marking the centers on *both* long edges.

2. Using the pattern as a guide, cut 12 lengths of gold lamé piping. Fold each strip in half and snip-mark the center.

3. Matching centers and ends, machine baste the piping to each long edge of each full skirt panel and to the side edge of each front panel. Be sure to position the cord just to the left of the ½" seam line and use a zipper foot so you can stitch close to the cord in the piping. Since the edges of the skirt are not on the straight of grain, you may find it necessary to gently ease the skirt onto the piping strip. Use lots of pins to hold it in place for basting.

4. To gather each 3¾"-wide moiré strip, machine baste ⅜" and ⅝" from each long edge.

5. Pin a moiré strip to the outer edge of each velveteen front panel with centers and ends matching. Draw up the machine basting to fit. Pin, adjusting gathers evenly, then baste in place. Stitch from the skirt-panel side, using a zipper foot and stitching just inside the basting that holds the piping in place.

6. Add a tapestry panel to the remaining long edge of the moiré strip, being careful to adjust the gathers so they are parallel in the strip and do not slant across the strip.

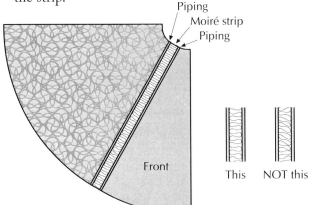

7. Join the remaining tapestry and velveteen panels with moiré strips in the same way, alternating the fabrics.

8. Serge, zigzag, or bind the raw edges of all seams and press toward the skirt panels, being careful not to crush the velveteen nap or melt the lamé piping.

9. Serge or zigzag the front and bottom edges of the tree skirt. Turn under and press ½"; edgestitch.

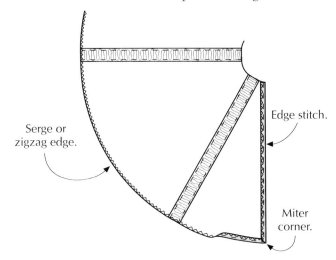

10. Position and stitch gold trim along the front and bottom edges, mitering corners.

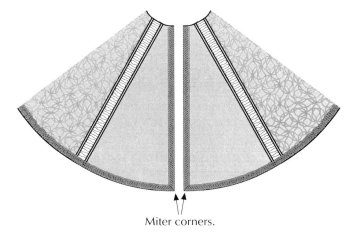

11. Join the 3"-wide bias strips of moiré into one long piece, using diagonal seams. Press seams open.

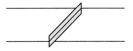

12. Fold the 3"-wide bias strip in half lengthwise, wrong sides together, and press. Fold in half crosswise and snip-mark the center at the raw edges.

13. Pin the bias to the upper edge of the tree skirt with centers matching and raw edges even. Stitch ½" from the raw edges.

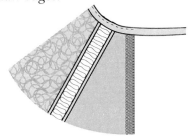

14. Turn the bias to the inside and hand stitch in place along the seam line. To finish the ends of the bias, turn the raw edge in and hand stitch the folded edges together. Turn in the raw edge at each end and tuck the cord of a tassel inside. Whipstitch the bias to the top edge of the tassel.

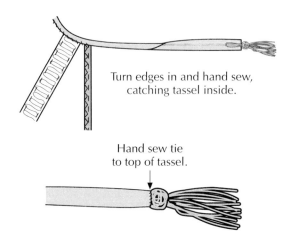

Turn edges in and hand sew, catching tassel inside.

Hand sew tie to top of tassel.

Tie the completed skirt around the base of the tree, over the tree stand. If necessary, tuck a scrap of the moiré inside to cover up the tree stand hardware.

Angel Tree Topper

Finished Size: 16½" tall

Make this regal angel to top your tree or dress up the mantel. Use a purchased ceramic head and make her dress from moiré. She's easier to assemble than she appears.

Materials and Tools

14" x 14" piece of plastic needlepoint canvas for supporting cone
¼ yd. polyester fleece for body, halo, and wings
¼ yd. of 45"-wide gold tissue lamé for halo and wings
¼ yd. of 45"-wide lightweight woven fusible interfacing
2½ yds. fancy gold trim for the halo and wings
½ yd. of 45"- or 54"-wide pink moiré faille for the gown
⅔ yd. of ¼"-wide pregathered white lace for sleeves and collar
2 chenille stems (pipe cleaner), each 12" long
18 small ready-made burgundy satin roses
¾ yd. of 1"-wide pregathered gold lamé ruffling for bottom of gown
¾ yd. of ½"-wide gold trim for bottom of gown
1 yd. of ⅛"-wide burgundy ribbon
¾ yd. *each* of ⅛"-wide green and pink ribbon
1⅜ yds. narrow gold ribbon or trim
3" ceramic doll head with separate hands*
White cord or heavy thread
Tapestry needle
Glue gun and glue

*This measurement is from the top of the head to the bottom edge of the shoulders.

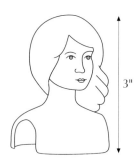

3"

Assembly

Use the patterns on pages 26–27 and the cone pattern on pullout pattern sheet #3. Refer to photo on page 8.

Body

1. Cut the cone shape for the body from the plastic needlepoint canvas.
2. Thread the tapestry needle with an 18" length of cord.
3. Shape the piece into a cone by overlapping the long edges about ½" and whipstitch together with the cord. The top of the cone should measure approximately 1" across the center, and the bottom should measure approximately 4" across the center.

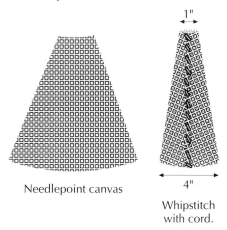

Needlepoint canvas

Whipstitch with cord.

4. Cut a 4" x 8" piece from the polyester fleece and fold in half crosswise. Then gather into a ball and, working from the bottom of the cone, stuff the fleece into the neck. It should fit very snugly. If not, add another layer of fleece.

Polyester fleece

5. Make sure the cone stands securely without tipping. If not, trim the bottom edges as needed to make it sit straight. Set cone aside.

Halo and Wings

1. Following manufacturer's instructions, apply the fusible interfacing to the wrong side of the gold lamé.
2. Cut 2 halos and 2 pairs of wings from the lamé. Cut 1 halo and 1 pair of wings from the polyester fleece. Machine baste the fleece to the wrong side of 1 halo and 1 wing, stitching ⅛" from the raw edge.

3. With right sides facing, stitch the 2 halos and the 2 wings together, leaving an opening for turning where indicated on the pattern pieces. Clip the inner curves and corners on the wing piece. Turn halo and wing right side out and finger-press the outer edges, turning in the seam allowance at the opening edges. Whipstitch edges closed.

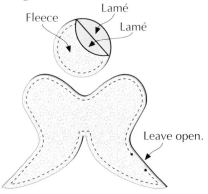

Lamé

Fleece

Lamé

Leave open.

4. Pin gold trim to the outer edge of the halo and the wing, turning under the edge where the ends meet. Machine stitch in place. Repeat on the other side of the halo and wings. Set aside.

Add trim to both sides of halo and wings.

Gown

1. From the pink moiré, cut the following:
   1 piece, 7" x 12¾", for sleeves
   1 piece, 13" x 24", for the skirt
   1 strip of bias, 3¼" x 10", for the collar
2. Turn under and press ¾" at the short ends of the sleeve piece. Edgestitch a narrow piece of the pregathered white lace to each end, tucking the edge of the lace under the turned edge. Machine baste ½" and ⅝" from each short end, beginning and ending stitching ½" from the long raw edges. Machine baste 4½" from short finished edges (not the bottom edge of lace).

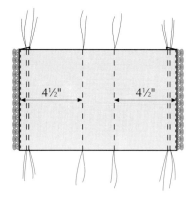

4½"   4½"

3. Draw up the gathering at each location as tightly as possible and tie off the threads. Machine stitch on top of the gathers.

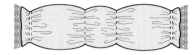

4. With right sides facing and long edges even, stitch ¼" from the raw edges. Turn the sleeve tube right side out.

5. Put several drops of glue from the glue gun into each hand cavity and push a chenille stem all the way into each one (a). Allow to cool. Thread the arms/hands through the sleeves (b). Tie a 6" length of burgundy ribbon around each wrist in a tight square knot. Glue a rose over each knot and trim the ribbon ends to ¾" (c).

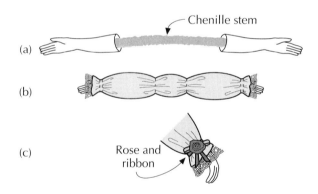

(a) Chenille stem

(b)

(c) Rose and ribbon

6. Tuck a small piece of polyester fleece into the hole in the doll's head, then add a healthy portion of glue from the glue gun. Quickly push the sleeve piece into the shoulder cavity, making sure the hands are pointing in the correct direction. Allow to cool and set aside.

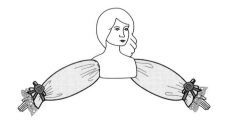

7. Turn under and press ¼" on one long edge of the skirt piece. Turn and press an additional ¼" and stitch. Tuck the raw edge of the pregathered lamé ruffling under the finished edge of the skirt and stitch in place. Position the ½"-wide gold trim even with the bottom edge of the moiré skirt and stitch in place.

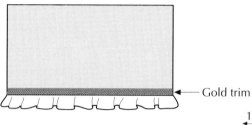

Gold trim

8. With right sides together, stitch the short ends of the skirt, beginning at the bottom in a ¼"-wide seam and tapering to a 1"-wide seam by the time you reach the other end. Trim the seam to an even ¼" and zigzag the seam allowances together. Press seam toward one side.

1"

Zigzag close to stitching.

9. Glue 15 satin roses to the top edge of the gold trim at the bottom edge of the skirt, spacing them 1½" apart.

10. Machine baste ¼" and ⅜" from the raw edge, beginning and ending at the seam. Pull the skirt over the prepared cone and draw up the gathers to fit the cone ½" from the top edge. Tie threads securely, then hand sew or glue the skirt to the cone.

Cone

11. Turn under and press a narrow hem on one long edge of the collar. Turn again and press. Position lace under the edge and edgestitch in place.

12. With right sides together, stitch the short ends of the collar in a ¼"-wide seam. Press seam open. Turn under and press ¾" on the remaining raw edge. Machine baste ⅛" and ¼" from the edge, beginning and ending at the seam.

13. Pull the collar over the doll's head and draw up the gathers to fit. Tie off thread ends securely. Glue a rose to the center front.

Finishing

1. Liberally coat fleece at the top of the cone with glue and put some inside the doll-head cavity. Quickly position the head on the cone, pushing it down securely. Allow to cool.

2. Cut the gold ribbon or trim in half and add to the green, burgundy, and pink ribbons. Tie all 5 pieces of ribbon and trim around the waist and under the collar in a square knot.
3. Glue the halo to the back of the head.
4. Hand sew or glue the wings to the back of the collar.
5. Bend the arms into a pleasing position.

Note: If you wish to use the angel as a centerpiece or on the mantel, fill the cone with a piece of polyester fleece to add some weight as this angel is top heavy.

Stockings
Finished Size: 11" x 15"

Two versions of this elegant stocking are shown on page 8—a simple one for him and a ruffled one for her. Directions for both versions follow.

Materials for 2 stockings

18" x 25" piece of cranberry velveteen
18" x 25" piece of tapestry
4" x 32" piece of gold tissue lamé
4" x 32" piece of lightweight cool-fuse interfacing, such as Touch of Gold
2½ yds. of gold lamé piping
2 gold drapery tassels, each 3½" long
2½ yds. each of ⅛"-wide gold and burgundy ribbon
5 yds. each of ⅛"-wide pink and light green ribbon
3½" x 24" strip of pink moiré faille for the optional ruffle
16"-long piece of ½"-wide gold braid for the stocking without ruffle

Cutting

Use pattern on pullout pattern sheet #1.

1. Cut 1 cranberry velveteen stocking piece and 1 tapestry stocking piece for each stocking. Make sure to cut the velveteen stocking with the pattern face up and the tapestry stocking with the pattern face down.
2. Cut 1 heel and 1 toe for each stocking from tapestry.
3. Apply the fusible interfacing to the wrong side of the tissue lamé, following the manufacturer's instructions at an iron temperature as low as possible to avoid melting or shrinking the lamé.
4. For each cuff, cut a 4½" x 16" strip of lamé.

Assembly

Note: All seam allowances are ¼" wide unless otherwise noted.

1. With raw edges even, machine baste the piping to the outer edges of the tapestry stocking, beginning and ending the piping 3" below the top edge of the stocking. Use a zipper foot to get close to the cord.

Repeat with the inner edges of the heel and toe piece. Turn the seam to the underside of the heel and toe and press carefully.

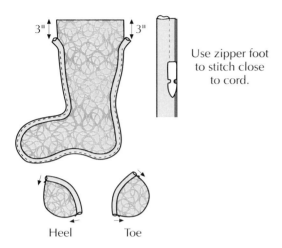

3"   3"

Use zipper foot to stitch close to cord.

Heel   Toe

2. Position the heel and toe on the velveteen stocking with raw edges even and stitch in-the-ditch of the piping seam. Machine baste around the raw edges.

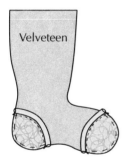

Velveteen

3. With right sides together, stitch the tapestry and velveteen stocking pieces together, using a zipper foot and stitching from the tapestry side, just inside the basting that holds the piping in place. Clip inner curves. Serge or zigzag the edges of the seam to finish. Turn the stocking right side out and press.

4. Fold the lamé cuff in half crosswise and stitch the short ends together, using a $\frac{1}{2}$"-wide seam. Press the seam open. Turn right side out.

5. *For the stocking with the ruffle:*
   a. Stitch the short ends of the moiré ruffle strip together in a $\frac{1}{4}$"-wide seam and press open.
   b. Finish one edge with serging or a narrow hem.
   c. Machine baste $\frac{1}{2}$" and $\frac{1}{4}$" from the remaining raw edge. Draw up the easestitching to fit the bottom edge of the lamé cuff. Pin and stitch. Press the seam toward the cuff.

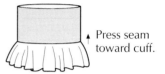

Press seam toward cuff.

   For the stocking without the ruffle, turn under and press $\frac{1}{2}$" along one edge of the cuff.

6. Pin the cuff to the top edge of the stocking *with the right side of the cuff against the wrong side of the stocking* and the seams matching at the left-hand side of the stocking. Stitch $\frac{1}{2}$" from the top edge and trim the seam to $\frac{1}{4}$". Turn the cuff to the right side and press.

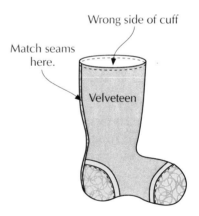

Wrong side of cuff

Match seams here.

Velveteen

7. *For the stocking with the ruffle,* pin the cuff in place just above the ruffle and stitch in-the-ditch of the ruffle seam. See illustration on the following page.

   For the stocking without the ruffle, pin the folded edge of the cuff to the stocking. Pin gold trim on top with one edge just covering the bottom edge of the cuff and stitch in place through all layers.

Securely hand sew the top of the tassel to the top edge of the cuff.

together and tie them in a single overhand knot, allowing a 3"-long loop to extend above the knot.

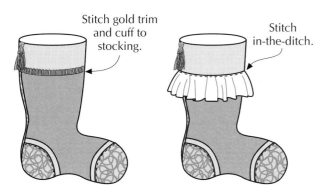

Stitch gold trim and cuff to stocking.

Stitch in-the-ditch.

3"-long loop

Overhand knot

8. For each stocking, cut a 1¼-yard length of gold and 1 of burgundy ribbon and 2 similar lengths of the pink and light green ribbons. You should have a total of 6 ribbons for each ribbon streamer. Group ribbons

9. Hand tack the ribbon streamer to the top edge of the stocking just in front of the tassel. Cut the ribbon ends at various lengths at an angle. (Hang the stocking by the ribbon and tassel loops.)

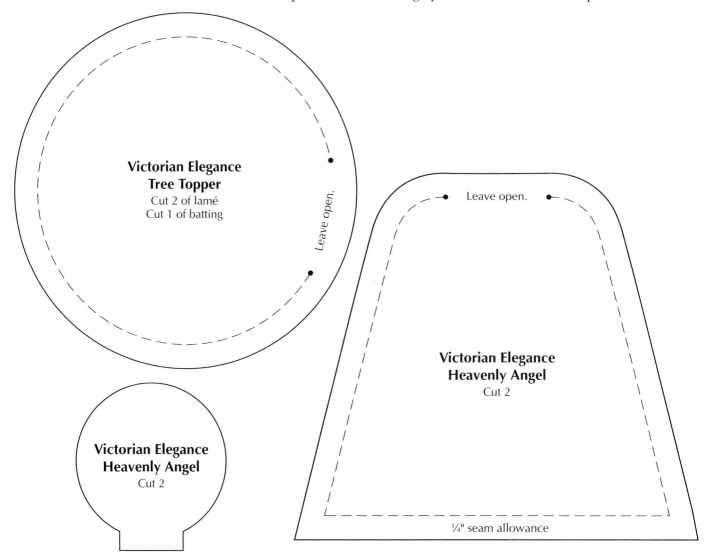

**Victorian Elegance
Tree Topper**
Cut 2 of lamé
Cut 1 of batting

Leave open.

**Victorian Elegance
Heavenly Angel**
Cut 2

Leave open.

**Victorian Elegance
Heavenly Angel**
Cut 2

¼" seam allowance

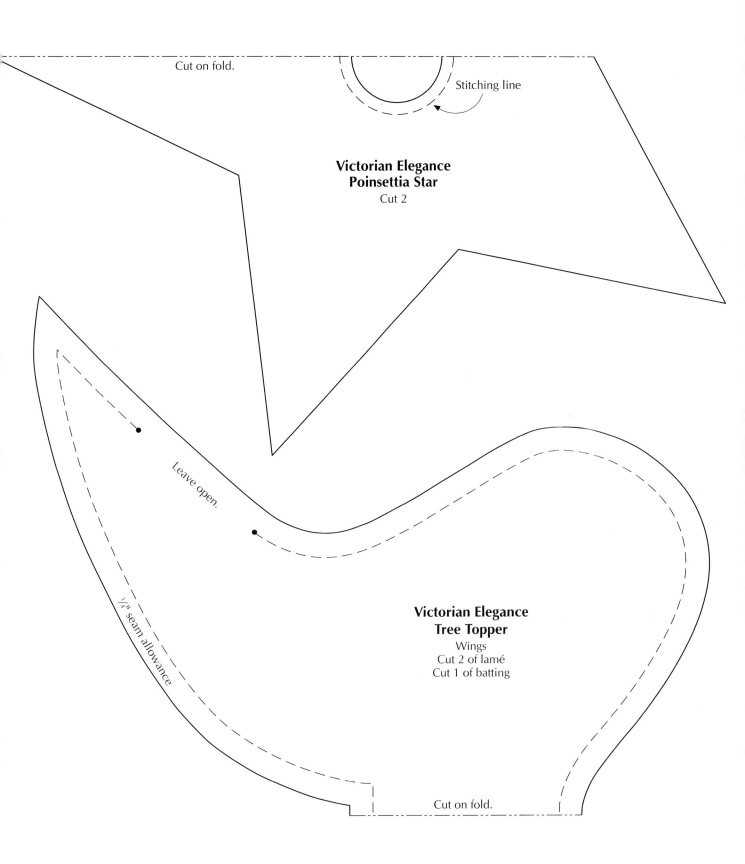

Cut on fold.

Stitching line

**Victorian Elegance
Poinsettia Star**
Cut 2

Leave open.

¼" seam allowance

**Victorian Elegance
Tree Topper**
Wings
Cut 2 of lamé
Cut 1 of batting

Cut on fold.

An Americana Christmas

by Christal Carter

◀ Give a Yuletide cheer for the red, white, and blue! Patriotic ornaments—drums and bugles, the stars and bars, and pinwheels—decorate the tree as well as a wall hanging and wreath for fanciful holiday fireworks.

Used as a spectacular tree topper, a shiny gold horn trumpets the season's greetings. Firecrackers, pinwheels, and miniature documents make wonderful no-sew ornaments. ▶

◀ *A glorious star trimmed with gold braid makes a festive tree skirt. Flags and the red–white–and–blue stocking ornaments are easy to sew.*

29

I designed this Americana Christmas theme with help from my decorating partners, Shirley Baker and Terri Dahmer. Reminiscent of golden sparklers and fireworks, marching bands and unbridled patriotism, this decor is meant to inspire the American spirit during the holidays and throughout the year. The wall quilt features Uncle Sam holding Old Glory and a pair of drumsticks amid a starry display of fireworks. A wreath, featuring a wooden Uncle Sam toy, also contains firecracker clusters, a drum, and gilded wooden letters. With a few changes in the assembly process, the reversible star-shaped tree skirt, embellished with gold braid, could also double as a table topper!

A unique treetop arrangement was formed around a large brass horn, with the addition of shining gold stars, curled gold wire tendrils, and a large ribbon cluster.

Handcrafted ornaments include drums, tasseled flags, firecracker bundles, patriotic stockings, and reproductions of historical American documents. Directions for these follow.

If you would like to add a table centerpiece to your decor, use a wreathed candle arrangement with a glass chimney and decorate with one or more of the handcrafted ornaments.

When Christmas celebrating has long passed, you can still enjoy the wall quilt and decorations for the Fourth of July—or throughout the year if it fits with your decorating scheme!

Trim-the-Tree Shopping List

- ✔ Large red glass balls
- ✔ Brass horns (small brass horn ornaments)
- ✔ Large gold star ornaments*
- ✔ Gold lamé Christmas balls
- ✔ Gold star garlands
- ✔ Red-and-white candy canes (ornaments or real ones)
- ✔ Gold wrapping paper and red ribbon or elastic ties for gifts
- ✔ Gold wire floral picks like those on the wreath
- ✔ White mini lights (300 to 400 for a 6' tree)

*If gold star ornaments are not available, cut stars from Styrofoam and spray paint with gold glitter.

CHRISTAL CARTER

Christal Carter is known for her wonderful Log Cabin picture quilts. Many of Christal's quilts have won prizes, and her work has taken her on teaching and lecturing tours throughout the United States and to Australia. She offers classes on her designs, as well as on making appliquéd picture quilts, decorating with quilts, and reviving thrift-shop quilts. She is also the author of three successful books featuring her quilt designs, *Holiday Happenings*, *Quilts for All Seasons*, and *A Child's Garden of Quilts*.

Christal owns and operates Majestic Seasons, a company that decorates for corporate and hotel theme parties and seasonal events. Her decorating skills came in handy as photo stylist for this book. Christal makes her home in southern California with her husband, Bill.

Star Tree Skirt

Finished size: 58" diameter

Six diamonds form this reversible, star-shaped tree skirt, edged in red bias tape and machine quilted. Gold braid echoes the star design and adds sparkle. To adapt this pattern to make a stunning table topper, eliminate the side slit and center hole. Add gold tassels to the star points for extra pizzazz!

Materials

2¼ yds. of 44"-wide navy blue fabric
2¾ yds. of 44"-wide off-white print
8 yds. of narrow, single-fold red bias tape
5 yds. of ½"-wide gold braid
60" square of quilt batting
18" x 30" piece of paper for template

Assembly

Use the drafting template on page 47.

1. Using the template as a guide, make a paper pattern for the diamond. Trace one of the 60° points (A) of the template in the lower corner of a piece of paper. Extend the 2 lines exactly 13" each from this point. Trace a 120° angle (B) at the end of the 13" line as shown. Using this angle as a guide, make a line exactly 13" long. To complete the diamond, draw another 13"-long line that is parallel to the first one. To check for pattern accuracy, make sure all lines are 13" in length. The 2 pointed ends of your

large template should each match the 60° point (A) of the diamond template in the book and the 2 side angles should match the 120° point (B) of the diamond template.

Tip: If you want a larger tree skirt, simply increase the size of the diamond by lengthening the 13" line.

2. Using your paper pattern, cut 6 diamonds from the navy fabric. Be sure that the straight grain of fabric runs from point to point as indicated on the template.
3. With right sides together and using ¼"-wide seam allowances, sew 3 pairs of diamonds together as shown. Now sew the pairs together, forming a star but leaving 1 seam open. Press the seams to one side.

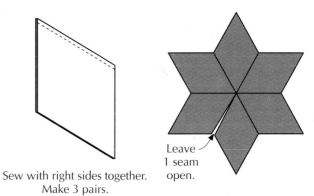

Sew with right sides together.
Make 3 pairs.

Leave 1 seam open.

To make your large diamond paper template, use template on page 47 and enlarge on paper. Cut 6 from navy blue fabric.

A
60°
Template
13"
B
120°
120°
B
13"
60°
A
13"
13"
13"

4. Using a white fabric marking pencil, mark the quilting lines on the completed star.

5. Cut and piece the backing fabric as shown. You will have excess backing fabric when you are finished, but this is necessary if the piece is to be reversible.

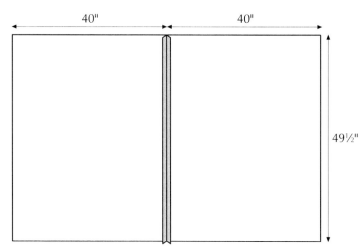

Piece backing fabric.

6. Layer backing (right side down) with batting and star top (right side up). Line up the backing seam with the star's open slit. Baste or pin layers together. You may trim off excess batting and backing at this time, but be sure to leave at least 1" of each extending around the outer edge of the star.

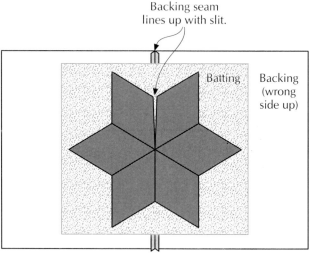

Layer backing, batting, and top.
Trim away excess batting and backing,
leaving 1" around star.

7. Hand or machine quilt the 3 layers together.

8. Trim batting and backing to match star top. Mark a 4"-diameter circle in the center of the star. Cut through batting and backing along the unsewn star seam and cut out the circle through all 3 layers.

9. To bind edges, sew bias tape to star top along edge, mitering the inside corners, then fold tape to back and sew in place by hand.

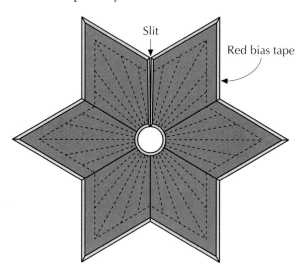

10. Using matching thread, appliqué gold braid in a star shape around tree skirt, placing it 2" from the outer edge and mitering the corners. Refer to the photo on page 29.

Note: To finish as a table topper, do not make the slit or the center hole; add gold tassels to the star points.

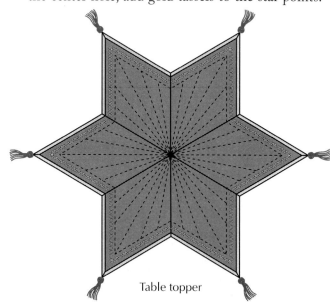

Table topper

Americana Wreath

Finished Size: 24" diameter

Supplies and Tools

7"-tall wooden letters: U, S, A
Gold spray paint
24"-diameter artificial pine wreath
Uncle Sam doll (page 34)
Flag ornament (page 40)
Drum ornament (page 42)
2 firecracker clusters (page 41)
1 yd. red braided cording
1 strand of 25 white mini lights
Gold wire floral pick*
Fine brass or gold-colored wire
Fine sandpaper
Glue gun and glue
Wire cutters

*These are sprays of 6–8 flexible gold wires attached to a pick. They resemble fireworks. If you can't find gold spray picks at your craft store, you can make your own by cutting three 24" lengths of brass wire and wiring them together in the center. Attach these to a stick (such as a bamboo skewer) or a piece of stiff wire and wrap the brass wire around a pencil to curl it.

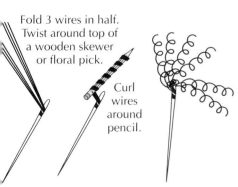

Fold 3 wires in half. Twist around top of a wooden skewer or floral pick.

Curl wires around pencil.

Assembly

1. Sand any rough edges on the wooden letters, then spray paint gold and allow to dry.
2. Attach Uncle Sam to the wreath by winding wire around the neck and through to the back of the wreath. Arrange arms holding a flag ornament and glue in place with glue gun. Arrange legs as desired and glue in place. (Refer to the photo.)
3. Wire the letters to the upper right side of wreath and use the glue gun to stabilize the letters.
4. Wire or glue the drum to the lower left side of wreath.
5. Wire the firecracker ornaments in place.
6. Drape the red braided cording over the letters and glue in place.
7. Wire the gold spray to the wreath as desired.
8. Carefully wrap the strand of mini lights through wreath, placing lights to show off ornaments.

Uncle Sam Doll

Finished Size: 14" tall

Materials, Supplies, and Tools

36"-long ½"-diameter wooden dowel for arms and legs
8"-long 1½"-diameter wooden dowel for body and hat
1 wooden popsicle stick for shoes
2"-diameter wooden-ball drawer knob for head
2 wooden beads, ½" diameter, for hands
6" x 12" piece of small-scale, red-and-white striped fabric for pant legs
1¾" x 5" piece of larger-scale, red-and-white striped fabric with stripes running along the 1¾" width for hat
4" square of heavy cardboard for hat brim
16 small brass screw eyes for knees and elbows
10"-long piece of gold cord for tie
2 gold crowns (found in craft stores)
2 gold jingle bells for tie ends
White craft glue
Acrylic paint: white, black, flesh, pink, red, and royal blue
Clear spray finish for wood or tole painting
Small piece of quilt batting for beard and mustache
American flag or flag ornament
Fine sandpaper
Small hand saw
Drill with small bit
Small paintbrush
Pliers

Assembly

Use pattern on pullout pattern sheet #2.
Refer to photo on page 33.

1. With saw, cut the 1½"-diameter dowel into 2 pieces, one 6" long for the body, and the other 1¾" long, for the hat.
2. Cut ½" diameter dowel into 8 pieces: 4 pieces, each 4" long, for arms; and 4 pieces, each 5" long, for legs.
3. Cut off curved ends of the popsicle stick, making each end 1¼" long, for the shoes.

4. Drill small holes in dowels as shown. Test a screw eye in hole to make sure holes are just the right size to get the screw eyes started.

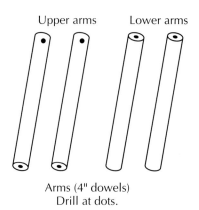

Arms (4" dowels)
Drill at dots.

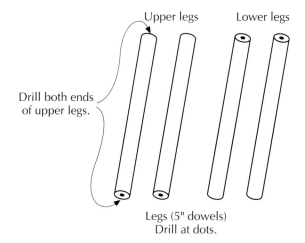

Legs (5" dowels)
Drill at dots.

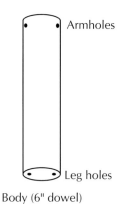

Body (6" dowel)

5. Lightly sand all wooden pieces: dowels, popsicle sticks, and drawer knob.

6. Paint 4 arm dowels blue, 2 hand beads flesh tone, 2 shoe sticks black, and the top of hat dowel red.

7. Paint body dowel and head as shown in illustration with step 10 below.

8. Mix 3 tablespoons of white craft glue with equal parts water and stir well. Set aside.

9. Cut small-scale striped fabric into 4 pieces, each 2¼" x 5". Make sure the stripes run along the length of the piece. Reserve a small scrap (1½" x 1½") for body.

10. Dip fabric into the glue mixture and wrap around the 4 leg dowels (5" pieces), overlapping the edges. Glue the 1½" by 1½" fabric piece onto body front with stripes vertical. If fabric hangs beyond dowel ends, trim to fit exactly. Let dry on waxed paper.

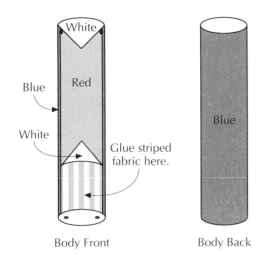

Body Front   Body Back

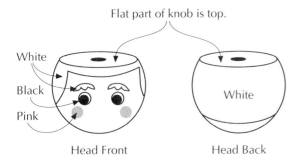

Flat part of knob is top.

White
Black
Pink
White

Head Front   Head Back

11. Dip the larger-scale striped fabric into glue mixture and wrap around the 1½" diameter dowel (1¾" in length) for hat, overlapping edges. If fabric hangs beyond the dowel ends, trim to fit exactly. Let dry completely.

12. For the hat brim, cut a 3"-diameter circle from cardboard; paint both sides and the edges red.

13. Using pliers, pry open 8 of the screw eyes. Hook each through a closed eye screw and pinch closed again.

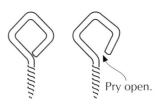

Eye screw

Insert open screw
into a closed one.

Close screw.
Make 8 pairs.

14. Screw the 8 screw-eye pairs into the leg, arm, and body holes.

15. Glue head, hat brim, and hat to body; glue hands to arms, and feet to legs.

16. Spray Uncle Sam with clear wood finish.

17. Using patterns on pullout pattern sheet #2, cut beard and mustache from the batting and glue to face.

18. Slip a gold crown over each end of the gold cord, then thread each end of the cord through the top of a jingle bell. Tie a knot at each end to secure.

19. Tie the cord in a bow around Uncle Sam's neck.

20. Glue the flag to one of Uncle Sam's arms.

Stocking Ornaments

Finished Size: 4" x 7"

Fill stockings with candy canes, small pinwheels, and toys to give as favors to guests.

Materials and Supplies for 8 stockings

½ yd. 44"-wide red-and-white striped fabric
¼ yd. 44"-wide navy blue print with white pindots or stars
3 yds. gold cording
16 gold crowns to top jingle bells. (Find these in craft stores in the jewelry-making section.)
16 gold jingle bells, ½" diameter
Glue gun and glue

Assembly

Use the pattern on page 47.

Tip: To "age" the red-and-white striped fabric, you may want to "tea dye" it by soaking it in tea before cutting.

1. Trace the stocking pattern onto paper and cut out.
2. Fold the striped fabric in half with right sides together. Using the stocking pattern, cut 8 pairs of stockings with the stripes running lengthwise.
3. For cuffs, cut 16 squares, each 3" x 3", from the navy blue print.
4. With right sides together and using a ¼"-wide seam allowance, sew a cuff square to the top edge of each stocking piece. Press seams toward cuff.

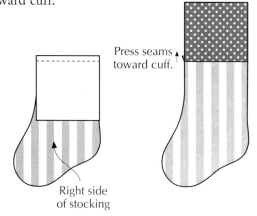

Press seams toward cuff.

Right side of stocking

5. With right sides together, sew a stocking front to a stocking back, leaving the top edge open. Clip curves to stitching line.

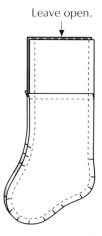

Leave open.

Layer stocking with right sides together.

6. Turn under and press ¼" along the raw edge of the cuff. Fold cuff down to cover the raw edges of the seam and stitch in place by hand, being careful not to let stitches show on the front. Turn stocking right side out and press.

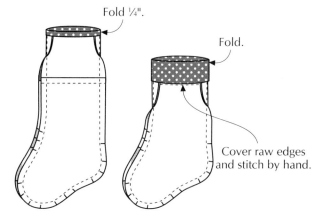

Fold ¼".

Fold.

Cover raw edges and stitch by hand.

7. Cut gold cord into 8 pieces, each 12" long. With glue gun, glue a gold crown and jingle bell to each end of each cord. Fold cord, not exactly in half, and tie a knot, leaving a loop at the top for hanging. Sew the knot in each cord to the stocking cuff.

Gold crown

Jingle bell

Historical Documents

Finished Size: 6" x 7"

These ornaments would be a great addition to the holiday table. Place one with the guests' names in calligraphy on each plate!

Materials and Supplies for 10 ornaments—
5 Declaration of Independence and 5 Bill of Rights

5 sheets of 8½" x 11" copy machine paper in tan or
    parchment color
10 bamboo hors d'oeuvres skewers, each 5½" long
20 wooden beads, ⅜" to ½" diameter
1 yd. of ⅜"-wide red satin ribbon
10 large gold sequins or small gold seals
White craft glue
Gold spray paint
Fine brass wire
Small paintbrush
Aluminum foil or waxed paper

Assembly

1. Make 5 photocopies of each document sheet found on page 38, using the tan or parchment-colored paper. Cut out each document around black lines.
2. Mix several tablespoons of white craft glue with equal parts of water. Using paintbrush, brush glue mixture onto both sides of each document. Let dry completely on cookie sheets covered with waxed paper or foil.
3. Glue a bead to each end of bamboo skewers. Allow glue to dry, then spray paint gold.
4. When documents and beaded skewers are dry, glue top edge of document to skewer, rolling it over to cover raw edges of paper.

5. Cut ribbon into 20 pieces, each 1½" long, angling the cut. Then glue 2 ribbons to lower left-hand side of each document. Glue gold sequin or gold seal over top raw edges of ribbon.

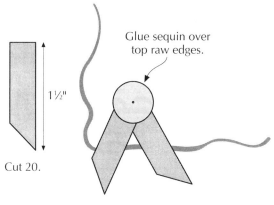

1½"

Cut 20.

Glue sequin over
top raw edges.

6. Cut 10 pieces of wire, each 8" long. Wire one to the top of each document, twisting wire around skewer near each end.

7. Before hanging documents on the tree, roll them carefully over a small cardboard tube or kitchen baster to give added shape.

Patriotic Pinwheels

Finished Size: 5½" diameter

These pinwheels would make a wonderful garland for a window or doorway!

Materials, Supplies, and Tools for 14 pinwheels

⅓ yd. 44"-wide red pinstripe fabric
⅓ yd. 44"-wide navy blue fabric with white stars or dots
⅓ yd. of 18"-wide paper-backed fusible web, such as Wonder-Under
14 small wooden stars, approximately ¾" to 1" across
Gold spray paint
Nylon fishing line
White craft glue
Aluminum foil or waxed paper
Large-eyed needle
Glue gun

Assembly

1. Following manufacturer's directions, apply the fusible web to the wrong side of the navy blue print.
2. Peel off the paper backing. Save the paper backing.
3. Cut the red pinstriped fabric into 14 squares, each 5½" x 5½". Then cut each square into 4 triangles as shown.

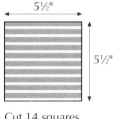

Cut 14 squares.

Cut each square into 4 triangles.

4. Place the triangles right side up on the wrong side of the navy blue print next to the applied fusible web. Arrange triangles into squares with stripes lined up as shown in illustration above right. You will have 2 sets of squares, each with a different striped pattern. Following manufacturer's directions, fuse in place, being careful not to get the fusible web on your iron. Use the paper backing you set aside earlier as a "press cloth."

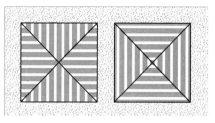

7 pinwheels will look like this.   7 pinwheels will look like this.

Place all 14 squares back on fusible web on navy print and fuse in place.

5. Cut out each square along the outer edges.
6. Mix ¼ cup white craft glue with ¼ cup water. Dip fabric squares into mixture to coat both sides lightly and let dry on foil or waxed paper.

7. When squares are completely dry, make 4 cuts toward the center, each 2½" long and each extending from a corner. *Do not cut all the way to the center!*

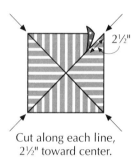

2½"

Cut along each line, 2½" toward center.

8. Fold alternating triangle point toward the center of the square and glue the points in place with a glue gun. These points will overlap.

9. Paint each wooden star gold and glue to pinwheel center with glue gun.
10. Thread the large-eyed needle with a 10" length of fishing line. Take needle through one of the pinwheel points to make a hanger. Knot the ends of the fishing line several times. Slide the knot to rest just behind the pinwheel point and glue in place.

Fishing line

Hide knot here.

Glue wooden star to center.

Flag Ornament

Finished Size: 3½" x 4½"

Use these flags as ornaments, part of the treetop decoration, and as package decorations, favors, and place cards.

Materials, Supplies, and Tools for 8 flags

⅓ yd. small-scale, red-and-white striped fabric for flags
⅓ yd. muslin for flag backing
⅛ yd. medium blue print with small white dots or stars for flags
⅓ yd. thin cotton batting
⅛ yd. paper-backed fusible web, such as Wonder-Under
72" of ¼"-diameter wooden doweling for flagpoles
8 wooden beads, ½" in diameter, for tops of flagpoles
2-ply heavy metallic gold thread for tassels OR 8 tassels, each about 1½" long
Gold spray paint
Nylon fishing line
Glue gun and glue
Small saw to cut dowels

Assembly

Tip: To "age" the red-and-white striped fabric, you may want to "tea dye" it by soaking it in tea before cutting.

1. Cut 8 rectangles, each 4" x 5", from the red-and-white striped fabric, the muslin, and the batting. The stripes should run along the 5" length.
2. Following manufacturer's directions, apply the fusible web to the wrong side of the blue print. Peel away the paper backing and discard. Cut 8 blue rectangles, each 2" x 2¼".
3. Place a blue rectangle, fusible web side down, on the right side in the upper left-hand corner of each striped rectangle. Fuse in place. For extra stability, you may want to zigzag stitch around the blue rectangle.

Fuse in place.

4. Layer each flag with a muslin rectangle, right sides together, and a rectangle of batting on top. Using ¼"-wide seam allowances, machine stitch through all 3 layers, leaving a 2"-long opening at the bottom edge for turning. Trim points.

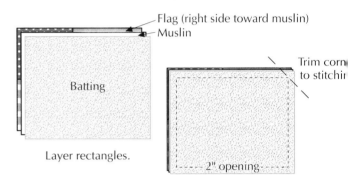

Flag (right side toward muslin)
Muslin
Trim corn to stitchir
Batting
Layer rectangles.
2" opening
Stitch through all 3 layers.

5. Turn flag right side out, making sure to poke out the corners. Slipstitch the opening closed by hand.
6. Cut dowels into 8 pieces, each 8½" long. With a glue gun, glue a bead to one end of each dowel. Allow glue to dry, then spray paint flagpoles gold. Allow to dry.
7. To make tassels, cut a piece of cardboard 2½" square. Wrap the gold thread around the cardboard at least 20 times. Cut a 5" piece of gold thread and slip under the thread on cardboard. Tie tightly around threads, making 2 or 3 knots. Cut through all wrapped threads along bottom edge of the cardboard. Wrap an 8"-long piece of gold thread around the top of the tassel about

⅓" down from the top. Knot 2 or 3 times to secure. Trim tassel ends to an even length.

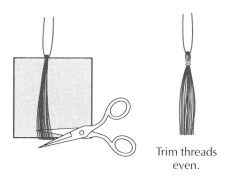

Trim threads even.

8. Using a needle and gold thread, sew flag to flagpole and tassel to top of flagpole just under bead at top.
9. Using a needle threaded with nylon fishing line, pierce upper left-hand corner of fabric to make a hanger. Knot fishing line several times to secure.

Fishing line

Firecracker Clusters

Finished Size: 4" tall

Use single firecrackers as favors or place cards, and in bundles to accent centerpieces and wreaths.

Materials, Supplies, and Tools for 8 ornaments

⅛ yd. navy blue print with white stars
¼ yd. red-and-white striped fabric
24"-long piece of ½"-diameter wood doweling
28"-long piece of ¾"-diameter wood doweling
32"-long piece of 1"-diameter wood doweling
1 yd. red elasticized cord for fuses
Small spool of 24-gauge brass wire
3 yds. gold cord or narrow ribbon to tie firecracker bundles together
Nylon fishing line
Spray adhesive
Fine sandpaper
Drill with small bit
Small saw to cut dowels
Glue gun and glue

Assembly

Tip: To "age" the red-and-white striped fabric, you may want to "tea dye" it by soaking it in tea before cutting.

1. From the navy blue print, cut 8 squares, each 3" x 3". From the red striped fabric, cut 8 squares, each 3½" x 3½", and 8 squares, each 4" x 4".

2. From each size of wooden doweling, cut 8 pieces in the following lengths:
   ½" diameter: 3"-long pieces
   ¾" diameter: 3½"-long pieces
   1" diameter: 4"-long pieces
3. Drill a small hole in the top of each piece of doweling. The elastic cord should just fit inside as a wick.
4. Sand dowels lightly if needed.
5. Lay a few fabric squares out on newspaper, right side down. Spray with adhesive and wrap around dowels, overlapping edges. The navy blue squares are for the smallest dowels, and the red striped squares are for the 2 larger-sized dowels. Stripes may go either direction on the dowels. Allow to dry completely. Continue until all dowels are covered.
6. Cut elastic cord into 24 pieces, each 1½" long.
7. Cut 48 pieces of wire, each 10" long. Wrap each around a pencil to make curlicues.
8. Using the glue gun, glue 2 curlicues and 1 wick into the drilled hole of each firecracker.
9. Arrange firecrackers in clusters of 3, one of each size, with the larger one to the back. Use the glue gun to glue clusters together, hiding fabric seams as you go.

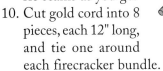

10. Cut gold cord into 8 pieces, each 12" long, and tie one around each firecracker bundle.
11. Cut the fishing line into desired lengths, fold in half, and glue to the back of each firecracker bundle to use as a hanger.

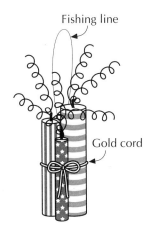

Fishing line

Gold cord

Drums
Finished Size: 3" x 4"

If you wish, add drums to wreaths and centerpieces or to the dining table as favors. Make a large one to match as a centerpiece.

Materials and Supplies for 16 drums

1 yd. red-and-white striped fabric
¾ yd. navy blue fabric with small white stars or dots
12 yds. of ½"-wide gold braid
12 yds. of ⅛"-wide gold middy braid
16 bamboo hors d'oeuvres skewers, each 8" or longer, for drumsticks
48" of 4"-diameter Styrofoam cylinders for drums
32 wooden beads, ½" in diameter, for drumsticks
32 rubber bands
Small package dressmaker pins (with flat pinheads)
Gold spray paint
White craft glue
Large-eyed needle
Nylon fishing line
Serrated kitchen knife
Glue gun and glue

Assembly

Tip: To "age" the red-and-white fabric, you may want to "tea dye" it by soaking it in tea before cutting.

1. From red striped fabric, cut 16 rectangles, each 3" x 13½", with stripes running lengthwise.
2. From navy blue fabric, cut 32 circles, each 5½" in diameter.
3. Cut Styrofoam into 16 pieces, each 3" long, using a serrated kitchen knife.
4. Mix ½ cup white craft glue with ½ cup water. Dip 16 of the navy blue circles in the mixture and drape over drum tops, covering completely. Secure with rubber bands and allow to dry completely. Repeat the process with the drum bottoms. (Rubber bands need not be removed.) See illustration with step 5.

5. Dip red striped fabric rectangles into glue mixture and wrap around drum sides, overlapping ends. Allow to dry completely.

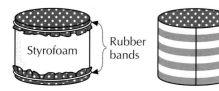

Styrofoam

Rubber bands

6. Cut 16 pieces of ⅛"-wide gold middy braid, each 24" long. Using dressmaker pins and beginning at the seam, divide drum into 4 equal sections as shown at top of drum. Near drum bottom, divide into fourths again, but at points midway between pins at top. These points mark the zigzag design for the braid placement.

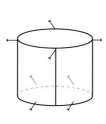

7. Beginning with the pin at the seam, attach one end of the braid to the Styrofoam at the drum top. Take braid down to the next pin at the bottom edge of the drum and attach with straight pin. Continue in a zigzag fashion around the drum and back to the beginning pin at the seam line, being sure to push each pin all the way into the drum.

Push pins all the way into Styrofoam.

8. Cut the ½"-wide gold braid into 32 pieces, each 13" long. Using glue gun, attach braid to top and bottom edge of each drum, covering pins and raw edges.

9. Cut bamboo skewers into 32 pieces, each 4" long. With glue, secure a wooden bead to the end of each stick. When dry, spray paint drumsticks gold. With glue gun, secure 2 drumsticks to the top of each drum.

10. Using the large-eyed needle threaded with nylon fishing line, pierce the top edge of the drum at an angle to make hanging loop. Tie the ends with several knots to secure.

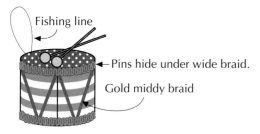

Fishing line

Pins hide under wide braid.

Gold middy braid

Tree Topper

Finished Size: varies with size of horn

Materials, Supplies, and Tools

Ribbon: off-white paper ribbon; gold metallic, red satin, or moiré ribbon; and fabric ribbon made from American flag fabric*
Gold wire floral picks**
3 large gold star ornaments
3 bamboo skewers
Large brass horn
Package or spool of floral wire
Wire cutters
Glue gun and glue

*To make coordinating ribbon from flag fabric or leftover pieces from ornaments, dip fabrics into a mixture of equal parts white craft glue and water. Let fabric dry and cut into widths as desired.
**These are sprays of 6–8 flexible gold wires attached to a pick and curled around a pencil. See illustration on page 33.

Assembly

1. Make a clustered ribbon bow. Using lengths of flexible floral wire, make individual bows from each of the ribbons, then wire all ribbon clusters together into one large bow.
2. Glue bamboo skewers to the back of each star and wire stars together.
3. Add curled gold wire sprays and stars behind the ribbon cluster.
4. Wire the horn to the treetop.

Note: Add flag ornaments to topper if desired.

Uncle Sam Wall Hanging

Finished Size: 26" x 62"

Materials: 44"-wide fabric

¼ yd. each of 4 similar dark blue prints for the sky and bow tie

¼ yd. red print for pinwheels and star points

Scrap of white print for shirt

Scrap of tan-colored fabric for face, hands, and drumstick ends

⅛ yd. medium blue print for flag and jacket*

3½" x 9" piece of black solid or print for shoes

¼ yd. of a second red print for drum, vest, and star

¼ yd. off-white solid for pants, hat, beard, flag, and drum

⅛ yd. red solid for pants and hat

⅛ yd. red pinstripe for flag

2 yds. navy blue print for border, binding, and backing

3 gold buttons, ¼" diameter, for vest

1 button or charm with clock motif for the pocket watch

Small gold beads for drum and small pinwheels

Small gold tassel for flagpole

2 star-shaped gold buttons or charms for star center and large pinwheel

1⅓ yds. of ⅜"-wide blue satin ribbon for flagpole and drumsticks

Black and white embroidery floss

28" by 56" piece of batting

*A print with white polka dots or stars on a blue background works well.

Cutting

From the 4 dark blue prints, cut:
23 squares, each 2⅞" x 2⅞". Cut 5 from 1 fabric and 6 from each of the other 3 fabrics. Cut squares once diagonally for 46 triangles.

From the remaining dark blue sky fabrics, cut:
135 squares, each 2½" x 2½"

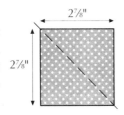

2⅞"

2⅞"

Cut to form 2 triangles.

From the red print for pinwheels and star points, cut:
20 squares, each 2⅞" x 2⅞"; cut once diagonally for 40 triangles

From the white print and the tan fabric, cut:
3 squares, each 2⅞" x 2⅞"; cut once diagonally for 6 triangles of each fabric

From the medium blue, cut:
1 square, 2⅞" x 2⅞"; cut once diagonally for 2 triangles
16 squares, each 2½" x 2½"

From the black, cut:
1 square, 2⅞" x 2⅞"; cut once diagonally for 2 triangles
2 squares, each 2½" x 2½", for shoes

From the red print for drum, vest, and star, cut:
17 squares, each 2½" x 2½"
2 squares, each 2⅞" x 2⅞"; cut once diagonally for vest

From the off-white solid, cut:
4 strips, each 1" x 25", for hat and pants
2 strips, each 1½" x 22½"
3 squares, each 2⅞" x 2⅞"; cut once diagonally for beard

From the red solid, cut:
    4 strips, each 1" x 25", for hat and pants
    2 strips, each 1½" x 22½", for flag

From the red pinstripe, cut:
    2 strips, each 1½" x 22½", for flag

From the navy blue print, cut:
    2 strips, each 2½" x 26½", for top and bottom borders
    1 strip, 2½" x 10½", for right pieced border
    1 strip, 2½" x 26½", for right pieced border
    1 strip, 2½" x 36½", for left pieced border
    1 strip, 2½" x 8½", for left pieced border

Assembly

1. Using ¼"-wide seam allowances and alternating the 1" x 25" red and off-white strips, make 2 strip-pieced units as shown. Press seams toward the red fabric. Crosscut each unit into 2 pieces, one 18½" long for the pants and the other 6½" long for the hat. You will have 2 of each length. Set aside.

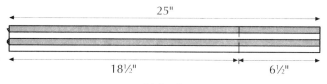

25"

18½"   6½"

Make 2.
Cut each into 2 sections.

2. Using ¼"-wide seam allowances and alternating the pinstriped and off-white 1½" x 23" strips, sew the long edges of the strips together as shown. Press seams toward the red pinstriped fabric. Crosscut the strip-pieced unit into 2 pieces, one 14½" long and the other 8½" long, for the flag.

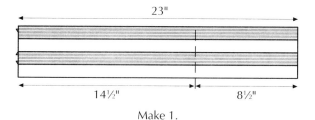

23"

14½"   8½"

Make 1.
Cut into 2 sections.

3. Assemble the flag, using 6 medium blue 2½" squares and the striped sections made in step 2.

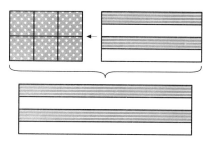

4. Following the diagram below, arrange all the pieces for the quilt top. Randomly place the dark blue squares in a pleasing arrangement.

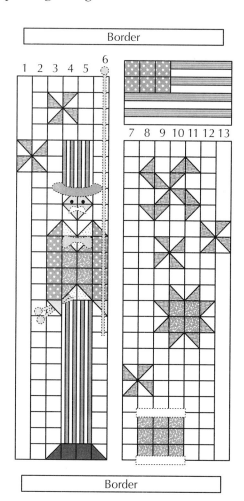

Background squares and triangles and border strips are assorted dark blue prints. Shapes with dashed outlines indicate placement for appliqué templates.

5. Sew pieces together in vertical rows.

Tip: *Press seams in row 1 up, seams in row 2 down, seams in row 3 up, and so on. This makes it easier to sew the rows together.*

6. Sew the vertical rows together in numerical order as shown in the illustration at the bottom of page 45. Sew the flag unit to the top of the unit made of rows 7–13. Add top and bottom borders last.

7. Cut two 5"-long pieces and one 35"-long piece of ⅜"-wide blue ribbon. Appliqué the 35"-long piece in place for the flagpole. See row 6 in illustration on bottom right of page 45. Pin the 5"-long pieces in place over the hand, then cut out excess ribbon covering hand triangle. Appliqué in place for drumsticks.

8. Using the patterns on pullout pattern sheet #2, cut appliqué pieces from the appropriate fabrics.

9. Referring to quilt plan for placement, appliqué tan circles to drumsticks. Appliqué red circle to top of flagpole. Appliqué red hatband to hat. Appliqué off-white top and bottom to drum, off-white mustache to face, and dark blue bow tie to shirt.

10. Using black embroidery floss, embroider a black outline stitch down the center of the legs. Embroider a black outline stitch to form Xs on the drum. Embroider eyes in black satin stitch. Using white embroidery floss, embroider a white outline stitch down the center of each shoe. Embroider shoelaces white.

Finishing

1. Mark quilt top for hand or machine quilting.

Quilting Suggestion: Quilt around Uncle Sam, flag, drum, stars, and pinwheels. Quilt Xs in background squares.

2. Cut batting and navy blue backing fabric into 28" x 56" rectangles. Batting and backing will be larger than the quilt top.

3. Layer quilt top, batting, and backing. Pin or baste all 3 layers together.

4. Quilt by hand or machine. Trim batting and backing even with quilt-top edge.

5. Cut 1½"-wide strips of navy blue print for binding. Sew binding to quilt front by machine, using a ¼"-wide seam allowance. Miter corners as shown on page 115. Fold binding to back of quilt and fold raw edges of binding under ¼". Sew in place by hand.

6. Sew buttons down vest front and sew pocket-watch button to vest. Sew beads at the points of the Xs on the drum and in the centers of the pinwheels. Sew a star-shaped button to the center of the large star and the large pinwheel. Sew the tassel to the top of the flagpole.

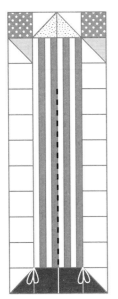

Embroider with black down center of legs, beginning 2 blocks down and ending at shoes.

Embroider laces and dividing line between feet with white.

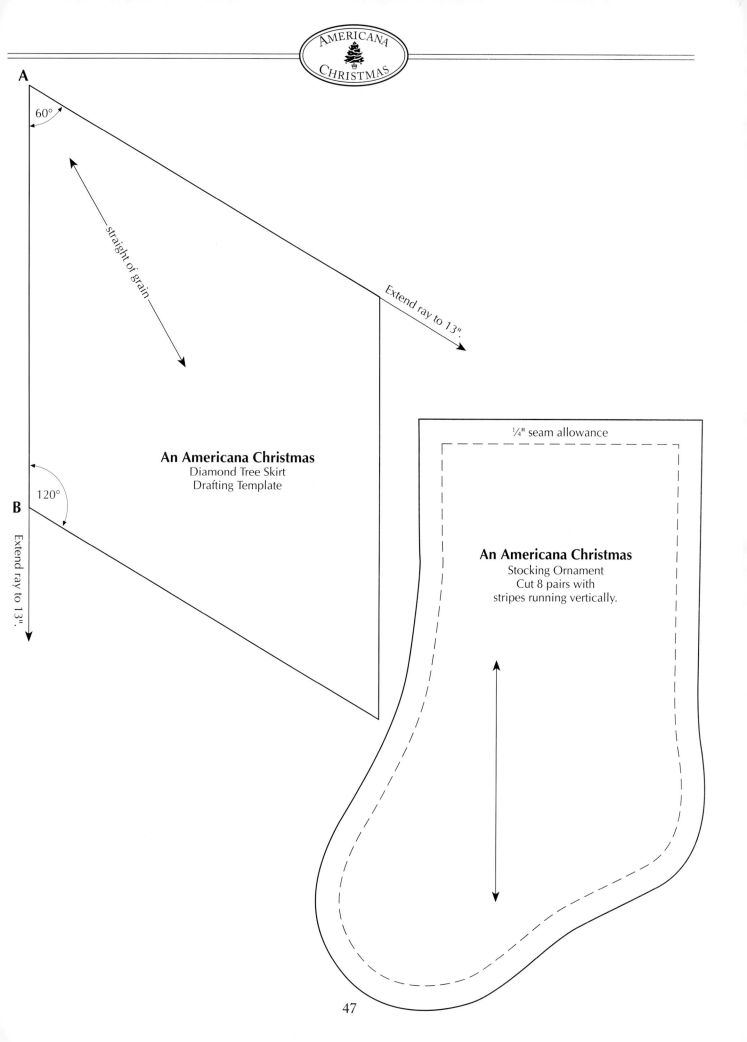

A

60°

straight of grain

Extend ray to 13".

An Americana Christmas
Diamond Tree Skirt
Drafting Template

120°

B

Extend ray to 13".

¼" seam allowance

An Americana Christmas
Stocking Ornament
Cut 8 pairs with
stripes running vertically.

Baltimore Nosegay

by Mimi Dietrich

As lacy and delicate as the bride doll under the tree, this nostalgic Christmas vignette is reminiscent of Christmases past. Ribbon roses, lace doilies, and bunches of dried baby's breath nestle in the branches. The Baltimore Nosegay motif is repeated on the tree skirt, wreath, stocking, and wall hanging. You will think of many other ways to use these beautiful ribbon and lace bouquets.

Feminine nosegays made of ribbon and lace nestle in the branches. ▶

A Christmas stocking, frosted with lace, is the perfect hiding place for holiday surprises, big and small. ▶

Softly shirred, this Christmas tree skirt adds a romantic finishing touch. ▼

Twenty years ago, the year before my first son was born, I designed "the perfect Christmas tree." It had red ribbon bows, red Christmas balls, little white lights, and one silver snow-flake. Ever since then, our trees have been covered with tradi-tional collections of all kinds of decorations—some of them handmade by my sons, many of them made by friends using quilting or cross-stitch designs. I've learned since then that those trees full of memories are truly the "perfect" Christmas trees!

I live in Baltimore, Maryland, and I enjoy teaching classes on appliquéd Baltimore Album quilts. When the antique Baltimore Album quilts were made in the 1850s, the ladies of Baltimore celebrated Christmas with an air of Victorian ele-gance. They decorated with ribbon roses, laces, and yards of ribbon. This year, I enjoyed designing this special Baltimore Nosegay Christmas Tree based on this practice.

If you have made a Baltimore Album quilt, appliquéd an Album block, or just dreamed about stitching one, come celebrate Christmas with this tree. Enjoy the elegance and simplicity of these gorgeous ribbon roses. I invite you to create a Baltimore Christmas memory of your very own.

To re-create the Baltimore Nosegay tree as shown in the photography, you will need to add glass ornaments in different sizes, plus long, slender icicle ornaments to provide contrast to the nosegays. (If you prefer a simpler, smaller tree, use only the nosegays and baby's breath for a tabletop tree.) For the tree topper, make an oversized bow from wire-edged ribbon and add baby's breath and pearl sprays. Wrap sofa cushions with ribbon, too, adding large bows for a coordinated accent.

Trim-the-Tree Shopping List

- ✔ White mini lights
- ✔ Cherry red and pink glass balls
- ✔ Silver and opaque white frosted glass balls
- ✔ Icicle ornaments
- ✔ Pearl sprays
- ✔ Wide wire-edged ribbon for tree topper
- ✔ Baby's breath
- ✔ Doll and teddy bear (optional)

MIMI DIETRICH

Mimi Dietrich is an award-winning quilter and the author of three best sellers, *Happy Endings*, *Handmade Quilts*, and *Baltimore Bouquets*. Her work also appears in *The Quilters' Companion*. She is a popular quilting teacher, whose workshops inspire students to share her enthusiasm and love for stitch-ing, particularly appliquéd Baltimore Album quilts. The inspiration for the tree in this book grew from her love for these quilts.

Mimi lives with her husband and two sons in Catonsville, Maryland. She has written articles for national quilt magazines and is one of the "Found-ing Mothers" of the Village Quilters in Catonsville. She is also a member of the Baltimore Heritage Quilters' Guild.

Baltimore Nosegay

Finished Size: 4" diameter

Transform shaded ribbon into beautiful rose decorations for a Baltimore style Christmas. These roses can be used as tree decorations, attached to packages, or included in wreaths and garlands for festive and elegant decorations. You could even wear one as a pin or hair ornament for holiday dress-up affairs.

Materials for 1 nosegay

12"-long piece of 2"-wide flat Cluny lace (or substitute a lace doily)
⅛ yd. green fabric for leaves
24"-long piece of 1½"-wide wire-edged ribbon, shaded from red to pink
1 yd. of ¼"-wide satin ribbon
Glue gun and glue
Tree ornament hooks

Assembly

1. Make the lace "doily," using the Cluny lace. With right sides together, stitch the short edges of the lace together in a ¼"-wide seam. Match the indentations on the scalloped edge of the lace and start stitching in that indentation. Don't worry if this slightly alters the length of the strip. Trim off the excess lace, leaving no more than a ¼"-wide seam allowance. Turn right side out.

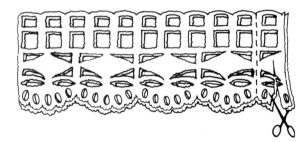

2. Starting on the right side of the lace at the seam, weave the 1-yard length of narrow satin ribbon in and out of the holes along the straight edge of the lace.

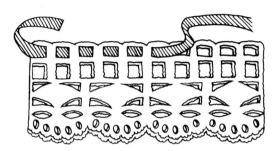

3. When you reach the starting point, gather up the lace with the ribbon, creating a circle. Tie ribbon ends in a square knot to secure, then tie a bow and trim the ribbon ends at an angle, leaving them long so they extend beyond the edge of the lace "doily."

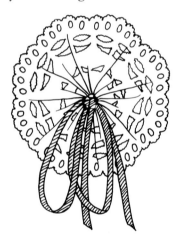

4. For the leaves, cut 5 rectangles of green fabric, each 2¼" x 4". Fold each rectangle in half, right sides together, to measure 2" x 2¼". Starting at the fold of the fabric along one edge, sew a ¼"-wide seam, backtacking at each end.

5. To create the leaf, finger-press the seam open, folding a small triangle at the top of the seam.

6. Turn the leaf right side out. The small triangle area will create a sharp point.

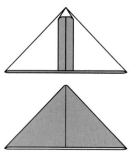

7. Gently press the leaf flat with raw edges even. Using a double strand of thread, do a running stitch through both layers ¼" from the raw edges. Begin the stitching on the right side of the leaf (the seamless side). Add the remaining leaves in a row, ending the stitching on the right side of the last leaf.

8. Draw up stitching, gathering leaves together tightly to form a circle. Tie a knot with the gathering threads to secure; clip the threads.

9. To make the ribbon rose, gently slide the ribbon on the wire at the pink edge of shaded ribbon to gather.

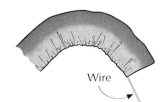

Wire

10. Draw up the ribbon along the wire from both ends, exposing the wire and gathering the ribbon tightly. Wrap the wire around the ribbon at each raw end as shown; clip the excess wire.

11. Starting at one end of the ribbon, form the rose by winding the gathered ribbon edge into a spiral. Thread a needle with a double strand of thread and sew the ribbon spiral in place, arranging the end of the ribbon under the completed rose. Shape the rose as desired, taking advantage of the wire edges to create a realistic flower.

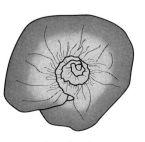

Underside of rose

12. Arrange the ribbon bow and streamers pointing down and apply a small bead of glue on the ribbon in the center of the gathered lace to hold the ribbons in position on the "doily."

13. Apply a circle of glue to the center of the lace. Place the green leaves on top of the glue. Gently press the green leaves in place to secure.

14. Apply a circle of glue to the center of the leaves and place the ribbon rose in the glue. Reshape the rose.

15. When the glue is set, turn the rose over and weave an ornament hook through the lace. Secure with a small amount of glue if desired.

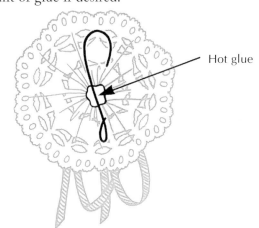

Hot glue

Baltimore Nosegay Tree Skirt

Finished Size: 20" diameter

Make this elegant tree skirt to complement your Baltimore Nosegay Christmas tree.

Materials: 44"-wide fabric

1 yd. red fabric for skirt
1 yd. white fabric for lining
3½ yds. of 2"-wide pregathered Cluny lace
5 yds. of 2-cord shirring tape (available in the drapery department of your fabric shop)
½ yd. of ¼"-wide red satin ribbon
7 Baltimore Nosegays (See directions on page 51.)
7 large safety pins

Assembly

1. Cut circles of red and white fabric, using the following method: Fold and press the red fabric in half, then into quarters. Mark a small **X** at the center point.

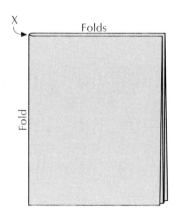

2. Using a tape measure or yardstick, measure out from the center 1" and 18" and mark as shown to form the curves. Cut carefully through all 4 layers along these curves to cut a circle. Repeat with the lining fabric (or use the red skirt as a pattern to cut the lining). Set lining aside.

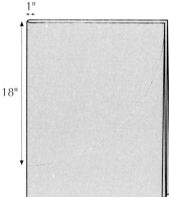

3. Cut along one of the crease lines of the skirt to create the opening.

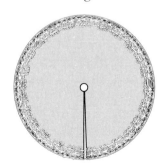

4. With right sides together, stitch the straight edge of the gathered lace to the outer edge of the red skirt, stitching ¼" from the edge.

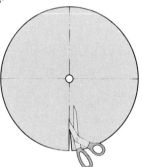

5. Fold the lining circle in half and then in half again. Press to crease the folds. Then fold each quarter of the circle in half and press the crease. This divides the circle into 8 equal sections. Cut along one of the folds to create the opening.

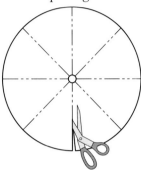

6. Cut 9 strips of shirring tape, each 18" long. Pin each strip to the right side of the lining along a crease. Pin the remaining 2 strips ¼" from the cut edges. The tapes should extend 1" beyond outer edge of lining.

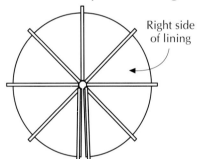

Right side of lining

7. Stitch the tapes in place, stitching along the edges and being careful not to catch the gathering cords in the stitching. With the sewing machine set for 20 stitches per inch, stitch around the inner edge of the skirt to secure the gathering cords. Backstitch over each cord, making sure the needle pierces each one to hold it securely.

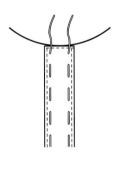

8. At the outer edge of the skirt, unlace a 2" length of each cord and pin each one up and out of the way.

9. With right sides together, carefully pin the lining to the skirt with outer raw edges matching. Stitch ¼" from the raw edges, leaving a 6" opening on one of the straight edges. Trim excess tape that extends beyond the outer edge.

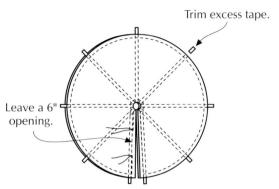

Trim excess tape.

Leave a 6" opening.

10. Turn the skirt right side out through the opening and press. Slipstitch opening edges closed.

11. Carefully smooth the 2 layers together and pin generously. Using red thread in the bobbin, stitch through the center of each shirring tape to attach it to the red skirt.

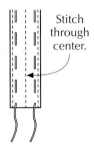

Stitch through center.

12. Sew 9" lengths of red ribbon to the skirt at the upper edge of the opening.

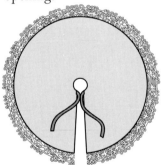

13. Draw up the gathering cords to expose 6" of cord at the end of each tape. Tie the gathering cords with small bows that can be released later so you can store the skirt flat.

14. Pin a nosegay to the skirt at each gathered area. Use large safety pins, pinning from the back of the skirt.

Baltimore Nosegay Stocking

Finished Size: Approximately 13" x 19"

Lace and ribbon roses let Santa know this is your special stocking!

Materials: 44"-wide fabric

⅝ yd. red fabric for stocking
1 yd. white fabric for lining and cuff
1½ yds. of 2"-wide flat Cluny lace
⅛ yd. green fabric for leaves
¾ yd. of 1½"-wide wire-edged ribbon, shaded from red to pink
1 yd. of ¼"-wide red satin ribbon

Assembly

Use the pattern on pullout pattern sheet #1.

1. Fold the red fabric and the white fabric in half and cut 2 stockings from each fabric. Cut 2 rectangles, each 6½" x 16½", from white fabric for the cuff. Cut 5 rectangles, each 2½" x 4", from green for leaves.
2. Using a ¼"-wide seam allowance, sew the red stockings, right sides together, leaving the top edge open. Clip curves and turn right side out. Press lightly. Repeat with the white stockings, but do not turn right side out. Slip the white stocking inside the red stocking and baste together around the top edge.

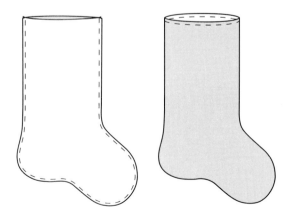

3. To make the cuff, fold each white rectangle in half, right sides together, and stitch ¼" from the raw edges. Press the seams open.

4. Cut a 1-yard piece from the lace and gather the top edge. Pin and stitch it to the right side of one of the cuffs with right sides together and raw edges even. Lap raw edges at seam.

5. Place the 2 cuff tubes right sides together and stitch ¼" from the raw edges to encase the lace. Turn the cuff right side out and press lightly.

6. To attach the cuff to the stocking, place the cuff inside the stocking with the right side of the cuff next to the lining, matching the cuff seam to the seam at the heel side of the stocking. Stitch ¼" from the top raw edges through all layers. Fold the cuff down over the stocking, allowing 1" of cuff above the seam line.
7. Make 1 nosegay, following the directions on pages 51–52. Hand sew the nosegay to the cuff. Stitch a ribbon loop to the back of the stocking for hanging.

Baltimore Nosegay Holiday Wreath

Finished Size: 18" diameter

Add a touch of elegance to your holidays with a wreath or garland decorated with nosegays of ribbon roses!

Materials

18"-diameter artificial "evergreen" wreath
3 yds. of 1½"-wide wire-edged ribbon, shaded red to pink
3 Baltimore Nosegays (See directions on page 51.)
Baby's breath
Glue gun and glue

Assembly

1. Prepare wreath. If it has been flattened by storage in the craft shop, separate the little evergreen stems so that the wreath has a pleasing shape.
2. Use the shaded ribbon to make a bow with 8 loops. Use a piece of wire to secure the bow and attach it to the wreath. Cut the streamers so they are 14" long.

3. Referring to the photo, use the wire edges of the ribbon to shape and arrange the streamers on the wreath.
4. Using the glue gun, attach the nosegays to the wreath.
5. Add sprigs of baby's breath between the nosegays and among the green stems.

Tip: Decorate evergreen sprays and garlands with bows, nosegays, and baby's breath, using these same techniques. Ribbons and nosegays also make great package decorations for a truly coordinated look.

Credits

The fabrics used in creating the Baltimore Nosegay designs were hand dyed by Edith Tanniru of American Beauty Fabrics, 610 Hamilton Parkway, DeWitt, NY 13214. The colors are Christmas Red Crush, Christmas Green Crush, and Parchment Tea Dye.

The wire-edged ribbon was provided by Quilters' Resource, Inc. It is from their Elegance Ribbon Collection.

Christmas Memories Wall Hanging

Finished size: 17½" x 17½"

Make three ribbon rose nosegays to add to the center of this small quilted wall hanging. Someone special, who shares your memories, would surely love to receive one as a gift.

Materials: 44"-wide fabric

1 yd. tea-dyed fabric for background and backing
⅛ yd. red fabric for border
½ yd. green fabric for borders, binding, and leaves
½ yd. of 2"-wide flat Cluny lace
1½ yds. of 1½"-wide wire-edged ribbon, shaded red to pink
20" x 20" piece of batting
Fine-line permanent pen

Cutting

From tea-dyed fabric, cut:
1 square, 9½" x 9½"
2 squares, each 8" x 8"; cut each one once diagonally to make 4 corner triangles.

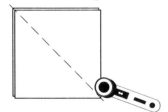

Save the remaining fabric for the quilt backing.

From red fabric, cut:
2 strips, each 1" x 9½"
2 strips, each 1" x 10½"
From green fabric, cut:
2 strips, each 2" x 42", for binding

2 strips, each 2" x 14½", for border
2 strips, each 2" x 17½", for border
6 pieces, each 2½" x 4", for leaves

Assembly

All seam allowances are ¼" wide.

1. Fold the 9½" center square in quarters diagonally and crease lightly.

2. Match the fold lines of the fabric to the pattern guidelines on page 59. Trace the words onto the fabric, using the fine-line permanent pen.

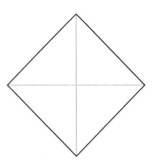

Tip: Photocopy the pattern so that you can use it on a light box. Iron a piece of freezer paper to the wrong side of the fabric. This will stabilize the fabric while you write.

3. Using ¼"-wide seams, sew the 1" x 9½" red border strips to opposite sides of the center square and press the seams toward the red strips. Repeat with the 1" x 10½" red strips.

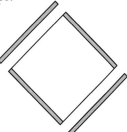

4. Sew a corner triangle to opposite sides of the square, then add corner triangles to the remaining sides as shown. Press the seam allowances toward the red strips.

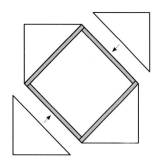

5. Sew the 2" x 14½" green strips to opposite sides of the wall hanging. Press seams toward green strips. Add the 2" x 17½" green strips the same way.

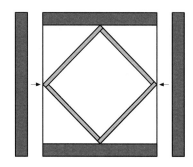

6. Trace the quilting designs on pullout pattern sheet #1 in the corners of the center square and in the corner triangles.

7. Layer the front, batting, and backing and quilt the traced designs. Also quilt in-the-ditch on each side of red strips and along inner edge of green borders.

8. Using the 2" x 42" green fabric strips, bind the edges.

9. To make the lace "doily" center, sew the short ends of the lace together to form a circle. Gather the straight edge of the lace by running a piece of quilting thread through the flat edge. Pull on the quilting thread to gather the inner edge of the lace. There should be an opening in the center. Tie the thread ends securely.

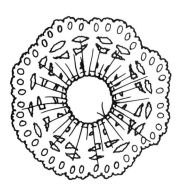

10. Carefully pin the lace "doily" to the center of the quilt top. Using a blind stitch, sew the edges of the lace to the quilt.

11. Following the nosegay directions on pages 51–52, make 6 leaves. Sew them into a circle. (As with the lace "doily," there will be an open space in the center.)

12. Cut the wire-edged ribbon into three 15" pieces. Following the directions on page 52, make 3 small roses. Stitch them in place in the center of the quilt.

BALTIMORE
NOSEGAY

Memory is the power to gather roses in Winter

Christmas Memories 1994

59

Christmas Garden
By Debbie Mumm

◀ Easy to appliqué, these gardener's stockings are ready to fill with surprises from the latest seed catalogs for your favorite gardener.

A splendid bouquet of silk sunflowers tied with raffia makes a fitting tree topper. ▼

◀ Garden lovers everywhere will appreciate this whimsical Christmas tribute. Seed packets, bunnies, sunflowers, birds, gardening tools, and a bumper crop of fruits and vegetables are a no-sew snap to cultivate as ornaments. Silk sunflowers, birds and nests, and raffia and berry garlands complete this warm, sunny scene.

◀ Cultivate a wheelbarrow full of these easy-to-make decorations. Hang them on the tree, use them to decorate packages, or string them together into a garland for the fireplace.

The gardening look is a very popular decorating trend! People are talking about their love of gardening with the same passion that quilters talk about quilting, so I thought the time was ripe to combine this fun, popular theme with the beloved traditions of Christmas. The techniques for these projects include quick-cutting, quick-fusing, and quick-sewing.

I used traditional deep reds and forest greens with antique tans, sophisticated golds, and black accents so my new gardening decor would complement my existing holiday decorations.

Directions are included for everything you need to create your own Christmas Garden Tree—a simple raffia garland and delightful No-Sew and Seed Packet Ornaments. To complete the look, add the coordinating Christmas Garden Tree Skirt and top off your tree with purchased silk sunflowers. Drape the mantel in a matching garland and hang the Gardener's Stockings with care. As you work on your tree and shop for materials, keep your eyes open for other gardening-motif ornaments to add, including birds, birds' nests, beehives, and small gardening tools.

Wrap your packages in economical brown kraft paper and finish off with a raffia bow and a personalized gift tag. Clay pots, potted poinsettias or silk sunflowers, candles in wooden or brass candle holders, wooden birds, and a stack of gardening books tied with a bow are all possibilities for expanding this whimsical garden scheme. For a simple door decoration, add a raffia bow to a rustic grapevine wreath.

Merry Christmas and Happy Gardening!

Trim-the-Tree Shopping List

- ✔ Silk sunflowers*
- ✔ Raffia bows
- ✔ Red birds*
- ✔ Greenery for the fireplace mantel
- ✔ Sunflower basket
- ✔ Wooden folk-art birds for the mantel
- ✔ Brown kraft paper
- ✔ Colored or amber mini or standard Christmas tree lights if desired. No lights were used on the tree in the photo.
- * If sunflowers and/or birds are too bright, dilute raw umber acrylic paint with water and daub onto the surface to tone it down. Use an electric hair dryer to dry them in a jiffy!

DEBBIE MUMM

Debbie Mumm is a quilt designer and illustrator who runs her own thriving pattern company, Mumm's The Word, in Spokane, Washington. Quilt enthusiasts know and respect the creativity and accuracy of Debbie's patterns. She has a devoted following for her creative, country-style designs. Her specialty is projects that feature timesaving techniques. Their small scale appeals to today's busy quilter. Quilt and craft patterns, calendars and stationery items, and books are all available with Debbie's signature look. Her first book, *Quick Country Quilting*, was released in 1991 and she is currently at work on another. Expect to see her name on a quilting video and her own line of fabric, too.

Debbie lives, surrounded by quilts, in her home overlooking Mt. Spokane, with her husband, Steve, and her son, Murphy.

The Gardener's Stockings

Finished Size: 12" x 23"

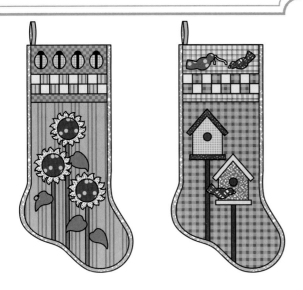

Sunflowers and ladybugs, birdhouses and blackbirds, plus a row of checkerboard decorate these fanciful, quick-fuse, holiday stockings.

Materials for 1 stocking: 44"-wide fabric

½ yd. for the lower stocking background, backing, and checkerboard

⅛ yd. for stocking top background and inner band below checkerboard

⅛ yd. for second color in checkerboard

⅜ yd. muslin

⅜ yd. cotton flannel

¾ yd. cotton for lining

½ yd. for hanger and bias binding

Several coordinated scraps or ⅛-yd. pieces of assorted printed cotton fabrics for appliqués

Heavyweight, paper-backed fusible web, such as HeatnBond

Cutting

Use the stocking pattern on pullout pattern sheet #2. Use the appliqué templates on pages 76–79.

1. Wash, dry, and press fabrics.
2. Using a rotary cutter, mat, and ruler, cut the following strips and pieces. Strip measurements are based on 42" of usable fabric width *after washing.*

From the fabric for the lower stocking, cut:
   1 lower stocking (Place pattern right side up on right side of fabric.)
   1 strip, 1½" x 20", for the checkerboard
From the fabric for the stocking top background, cut:
   1 strip, 3¼" x 8½"
   1 strip, 1½" x 8½", for band below checkerboard
From the second fabric for the checkerboard, cut:
   1 strip, 1½" x 20"

Note: Set the remaining fabrics aside for the appliqué and finishing steps below.

Stocking Front Assembly

1. With right sides together, sew the long edges of the two 1½" x 20" strips for the checkerboard together. Press the seam toward the darker strip.

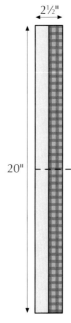

2. Cut the resulting strip-pieced unit in half to make 2 strip sets, each 2½" x 10". Sew the 2 units together and press the seam toward the darker strip.

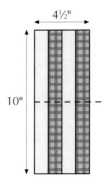

3. Cut the 4½" x 10" strip set in half and sew the resulting pieces together to make a 8½" x 5" unit. From that unit, cut 2 strips, each 1½" x 8½".

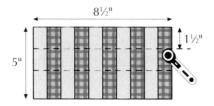

4. Pin and sew the 2 checkerboard strips together with light and dark squares alternating.
5. Sew the 1½" x 8½" background strip to the bottom edge of the checkerboard. Press the seam toward the strip. Sew the 3¼" x 8½" stocking top background piece to the top of the checkerboard. Press the seam toward the stocking top.

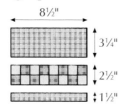

6. Sew the stocking top with checkerboard and band to the top edge of the lower stocking. Press the seam toward the band.

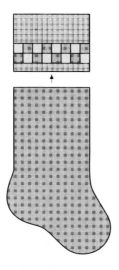

Appliqué

Refer to the "Fusible Appliqué" directions on page 74 and to the photo of the stockings (page 61) for appliqué colors and placement.

Sunflower Stocking

Use patterns on pages 76–78.

1. Trace 3 sets of petals and 3 centers onto the paper side of the fusible web. Trace 2 sunflower stems, then draw a third stem that measures ⅜" x 14".
2. Trace the 4 leaves, labeling them for correct placement when fusing. Trace 4 ladybugs for the top of the stocking.
3. Position and fuse the sunflowers to the lower stocking. Position the flower stems first, placing the left flower stem 2½" from the left edge of the stocking. Use the ⅜" x 14" stem for the center flower and position it approximately 4¼" from the left edge of the stocking. Position the right flower stem approximately 5⅞" from the left edge of the stocking. The ends of all 3 stems will extend beyond the bottom edge of the stocking. Trim the ends of each stem even with the raw edge at the bottom of the stocking.
4. Fuse 4 ladybugs to the stocking top background piece.

Birdhouse Stocking

Use patterns on pages 76–77.

1. Trace 2 birdhouses and 2 poles onto the paper side of the fusible web. Trace 2 birds that face left and 1 that faces right.
2. Position and fuse the birdhouses to the lower stocking, positioning the birdhouse poles first. Place the left pole approximately 2⅜" from the left edge of the stocking. Position the right pole approximately 5¾" from the left edge of the stocking. The ends of both poles will extend beyond the bottom edge of the stocking. Trim the ends of both poles even with the raw edge at the bottom of the stocking.
3. Fuse 2 birds to the stocking top, placing the bird with the worm at the left. Embroider the bird legs or use a fine-point permanent black felt pen to draw them. Fuse the remaining bird to the lower birdhouse.

Stocking Assembly

1. Press the muslin and the flannel to remove wrinkles. Cut a 13½" x 25" piece from each fabric. Place the muslin on a flat surface, add the piece of flannel, and then place the completed stocking front on top. Make sure everything is centered and that all layers are smooth and flat. *The muslin and flannel should extend*

¾"–1" beyond the edges of the stocking front. Hand baste through all layers around the outer edge of the stocking front.

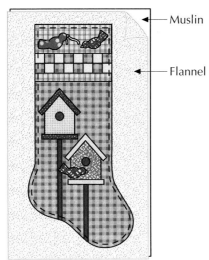

Muslin

Flannel

Baste stocking to
muslin and flannel.

2. Machine or hand quilt in the seam line on each side of the band below the checkerboard. Outline the appliqué designs by quilting ¹⁄₁₆" away from the edge of the designs. Quilt a 1¼" diagonal grid in the background behind the appliqué designs, but do not cross over the appliqués with the stitches.

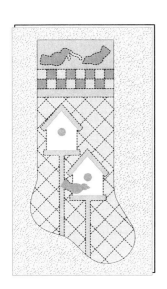

3. Trim the muslin and flannel so it extends ¼" beyond the raw edges of the stocking. *Trim even with the top edge of the stocking.*

4. Pin the wrong side of the completed stocking front to the wrong side of the remaining background fabric and use as a pattern to cut the stocking back, cutting along the outer edge of the flannel and muslin.

5. Fold the lining fabric in half, right sides together. Again using the stocking front as a pattern, cut 2 lining pieces.

6. With right sides together, stitch the lining to the stocking front ¼" from the top raw edge. Turn right side out and press the top edge.

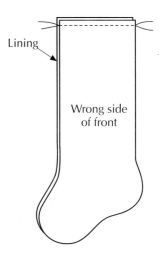

Lining

Wrong side
of front

7. To make hanger, cut a piece of binding fabric 2" x 5". Fold in half lengthwise, wrong sides together; press. Open the pressed strip and then fold each long edge in toward the center fold and press again. Topstitch along the edge.

8. Fold the hanger in half and baste to the right side of the stocking back, positioning it ½" from the top raw edge on the heel side of the stocking.

Stocking back

9. Sew the stocking back to the remaining lining piece as shown for the stocking front (step 6, page 65). Turn and press.

10. With the lining side of the completed stocking back face up on your work table, place the stocking front on top, right side up, with top and outer edges even. Pin and baste stocking together along all raw edges.

Finishing

Note: Follow steps 1–3 below to make your own bias binding or substitute 2 yards of double-fold, ready-made bias tape if you prefer.

1. Cut an 18" x 18" square from the binding fabric. Cut the square in half diagonally from corner to corner. From each half, cut 2 strips, each 2¾" wide.

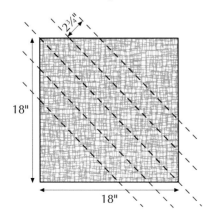

2. Sew the 4 binding strips together on the diagonal as shown to make one continuous strip.

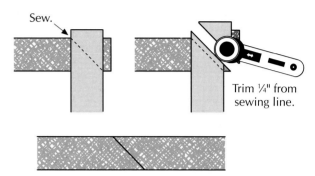

Sew.

Trim ¼" from sewing line.

3. Fold the bias strip in half lengthwise, wrong sides together. Press.

4. Pin the bias binding to the right side of the stocking front at the top edge of the right-hand side of the stocking. Make sure that raw edges are even with the raw edge of the stocking front and ½" of binding extends above the top edge. The flannel, lining, and stocking back should extend ¼" beyond the raw edges of the binding and the stocking front. Stitch ¼" from stocking front edge, going through all layers of the stocking and easing the bias binding around the toe and heel as you continue around the stocking. Be careful not to catch the hanger in the seam. Trim excess binding at other top edge, leaving only ½" of binding extending beyond the top of the stocking.

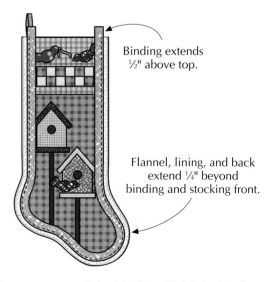

Binding extends ½" above top.

Flannel, lining, and back extend ¼" beyond binding and stocking front.

5. Press the seam toward the binding. Fold the binding over the edge of the flannel, lining, and stocking back, turning under the ½" extensions at the top. Press and pin in place. Hand sew the folded edge of the binding to the back of the stocking.

Seed Packet Ornaments

Finished Size: 3¼" x 4½"

Materials for 1 ornament

Scrap of fabric, 3¾" x 9"

Assorted scraps or ⅛-yd. pieces of coordinating printed cotton fabrics

Heavyweight paper-backed fusible web, such as HeatnBond

12"-long piece of natural jute for hanger

Dried flowers, baby's breath, and eucalyptus to fill the seed packet

Assembly

Use appliqué patterns on pullout pattern sheet #2.

1. Fold 3¾" x 9" seed packet fabric in half crosswise with right sides together. Stitch ¼" from the raw edges on each side. Leave the top edge open.

Fold

2. Turn right side out. Fray by pulling out threads for the first ¼" along the top edge of the "seed packet."
3. Trace the appliqué designs onto the paper side of the fusible web and cut out as described in "Fusible Appliqué" on page 74. Fuse each shape to the wrong side of the appropriate fabric and cut out.

Tip: When tracing letters, be sure to trace them in reverse as shown on the pattern page.

4. Fuse appliqués to the right side of a seed packet.
5. For the hanger, separate the 12"-long piece of jute into separate strands. Thread 1 strand of jute onto a needle with a large eye and tie a knot in one end. Thread the jute through the seed packet at the top right corner through both layers, working from the front to the back. This leaves the knot on the front of the bag. On the left side, thread the jute from the back to the front. Leave enough length for a hanger and tie a second knot in the jute. Trim ends.

6. Fill the seed packets with small stems of baby's breath, dried flowers, and eucalyptus.

Credits

Special thanks to:

Kelly Fisher, Jodi Gosse, and Angela Poole for piecing and fusing projects.

Kelly Fisher for technical writing.

Mairi Fischer for hand quilting.

67

Garlands

Finished Size: 9' long

Tree Garland

To make the tree garland, tie the end of several strands of natural raffia to the end of a red bead garland.

Materials

5 or 6 red wooden bead garlands, each approximately 9' in length
10' to 12' lengths of natural raffia

Tie a knot in the raffia around the bead garland every 10"–12".

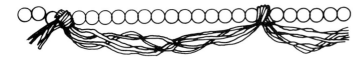

Fireplace Garland

Consider keeping this garland out all year 'round to decorate a country family room or kitchen!

Materials

9'-long fresh or artificial evergreen garland
9'-long red wooden bead garland
Natural raffia
4 No-Sew Sunflower ornaments (See directions on page 74.)
5 Seed Packet ornaments (See directions on page 67.)
Fine floral wire
Artificial silk sunflowers

Assembly

1. Make the garland as described for the Tree Garland above left.
2. Wire the raffia and bead garland to the evergreen garland at each raffia knot, being sure to hide the wire.
3. Arrange the garland on your mantel or drape it above as shown in the photo below. Add the Sunflower and Seed Packet ornaments. Embellish with sunflowers.

Finish the fireplace and mantel by adding pots of silk sunflowers or real poinsettias. Mix decorator gardening accessories and wooden birds with your greenery or add an earthy-looking grapevine wreath with a raffia bow.

◄ *Colorful raffia-and-berry garlands, embellished with sunflower ornaments, add a crowning touch to the fireplace mantel.*

Christmas Garden Tree Skirt

Finished Size: 31" x 31"

This tree skirt is made like a small quilt. After completing the tree skirt, adding the batting and backing, and completing part of the binding, you cut the slit and center circle, then finish the binding.

Since the look of this tree skirt is not strictly Christmas, wouldn't it be fun to use year 'round on a favorite large house plant?

Materials: 44"-wide fabric

1 yd. for background and outer border
⅙ yd. *each* of 2 fabrics for the checkerboard border
Several coordinated scraps or ⅛-yd. pieces for the appliqués
Paper-backed fusible web, such as HeatnBond
1 yd. for backing
1 yd. cotton flannel
½ yd. for binding
Rotary cutter, acrylic ruler, and mat
Seam ripper

Cutting

1. Wash, dry, and press fabrics.
2. Using a rotary cutter and acrylic ruler, cut the following strips and pieces. Strip measurements are based on 42" of usable fabric width *after washing*.

From the background fabric, cut:
   1 square, 26½" x 26½", for the skirt
      background
   4 strips, each 1½" x 42", for the
      outer border
From *each* checkerboard fabric, cut:
   3 strips, each 1½" x 42", for a total
      of 6 strips
From the binding fabric, cut:
   5 strips, each 2¾" x 42", for the
      outer and straight opening edges
   1 *bias* strip, 1½" x 16", to bind the
      inner circular edge (or substitute
      ready-made, double-fold bias
      tape in a coordinating color)

Assembly

Background

1. Fold the large square of background fabric in half, wrong sides together, and press. Fold in half again to form a square and press.
2. Trace the circle template on page 79 onto template plastic or heavy paper and cut out.

Tree Skirt Layout

3. Place the circle at the folded corner of the square, lining up the center cross hairs with 2 adjacent folded edges of the square. Trace around the outer edge of the circle, using a sharp pencil. This marks the cutting line for the inner opening. Also mark along one of the fold lines from the circle to the outer edge. *Do not cut yet.*

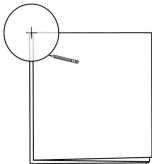

Checkerboard Border

1. Alternating the 2 fabrics, sew the 1½" x 42" checkerboard strips together along the long edges. Change sewing direction after adding each strip to avoid undue stretching. Press each seam toward the darker fabric before adding the next strip. Cut the resulting 6½" x 42" strip set in half crosswise. Each half should be approximately 21" long.

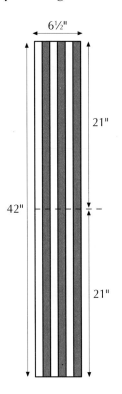

2. Sew the pieces together along the long edge to make a 12½" x 21" strip set.

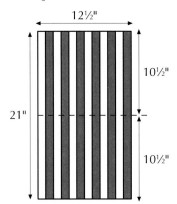

3. Cut the 12½" x 21" strip set in half again, creating pieces that are approximately 10½" long. Sew these pieces together to make a 10½" x 24½" strip set. From this strip set, cut 5 strips, each 1½" x 24½".

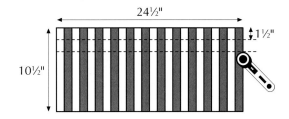

4. Using a seam ripper, carefully remove 2 sets of 2 squares from one 1½" x 24½" checkerboard strip. Set this leftover strip aside for step 5. Add 1 set of 2 squares to each of 2 of the remaining 1½" x 24½" strips to make 2 strips with 26 squares each. Pin these borders to the top and bottom edges of the background square.

   Stitch the checkerboard borders in place and press the seams toward the large background square. (See illustration with step 5.)

Tip: If the checkerboard border doesn't fit the edges of the square, take in or let out a few seam allowances ¹⁄₁₆" or less to make it fit the background square.

5. With a seam ripper, remove 2 sets of 4 squares from the leftover strip from step 4. Add 1 set of 4 squares to each of the 2 remaining 1½" x 24½" strips to make 2 strips with 28 squares each.

Pin checkerboard borders to the remaining sides of the background square, adjusting borders to fit if necessary as described in the tip with step 4 and paying attention to the color placement so the checkerboard pattern continues correctly at the corners. Stitch. Press seams toward the background square.

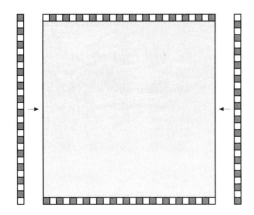

Outer Border

1. Sew the 1½" x 42" outer border strips to the top and bottom edges of the tree skirt. Trim excess border length and press seams toward the borders.
2. Sew the remaining outer border strips to the sides of the tree skirt. Trim excess and press.

Appliqués

Use the appliqué patterns on pages 76–77.

1. Trace the following appliqués onto the paper side of the fusible web as directed in "Fusible Appliqué" on page 74:

    4 birdhouses and poles
    3 sunflower pots
    4 birds facing left
    1 bird facing right

2. Cut out each appliqué, leaving an extra margin outside the lines. Fuse each appliqué to the wrong side of the appropriate appliqué fabric, then cut out on the marked line. Refer to the photo for color ideas.
3. Following the tree-skirt layout on page 69 for placement, position and fuse the birdhouse poles first. Use a long ruler to line them up even with the opposite corner of the tree skirt. Next, position and fuse 1 birdhouse at a time, then the flower stems, pots, flowers, and birds.
4. Press the completed tree skirt.

Layering the Tree Skirt

1. Press the backing and flannel fabrics, then cut them 4"–6" larger than the finished tree skirt.
2. Place the backing, right side down, on a smooth surface, then add the flannel and smooth out any wrinkles. Place the finished tree skirt, right side up, on the top of the first 2 layers. Make sure everything is centered and that the backing and flannel are flat. The backing and flannel should extend 2"–3" beyond each edge of the tree skirt.
3. Begin basting in the center and work out to the raw edges. Baste vertically and horizontally, forming a 3"–4" grid of stitching. Baste around each appliqué.
4. Baste or pin completely around the outer edge of the tree skirt. Trim the flannel and backing so they extend ¼" beyond the raw edges of the tree skirt.

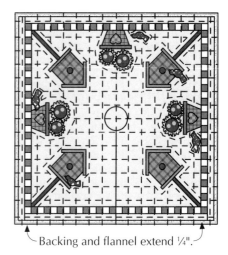

Backing and flannel extend ¼".

Finishing

Note: Quilting is not shown in following illustrations.

1. Press the five 2¾" x 42" straight-grain binding strips in half lengthwise, wrong sides together.
2. With raw edges matching, stitch a binding strip to the top and bottom edges of the tree skirt. See the illustration at the top of the following page. Stitch ¼" from the edge of the tree skirt, stitching through all layers. Trim away any excess binding and press the

seam toward the binding. *Do not trim the ¼" of flannel and backing that extends beyond the edge of the tree skirt.*

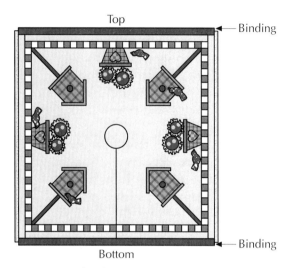

Sew binding to top and
bottom edges and press out.

3. Now cut on the marked line from the bottom edge of the tree skirt to the center hole. You will be cutting through the binding on the bottom edge. Also, cut out center hole through all layers as marked.

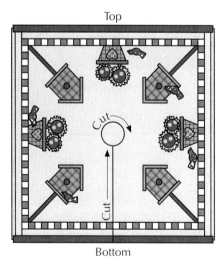

Cut along marked opening edge,
through binding on bottom edge
and around center circle.

4. To bind the center hole, press the 1½" x 16" bias strip in half lengthwise, wrong sides together. With raw edges even and right sides together, pin bias binding to the inner edge of tree skirt, easing as necessary.

Stitch ¼" from the raw edges. Trim excess binding strip even with the cut opening edges and press the seam toward the binding.

5. Sew binding strips to the sides of the tree skirt as you did the top and bottom edges in step 2. Trim away excess binding and press seam toward binding.

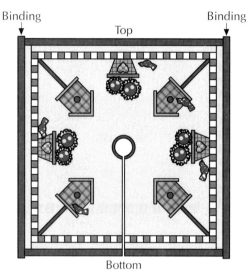

Sew binding to sides and press out.

6. Cut the remaining 2¾" x 42" binding strip in half to make two 21"-long strips. With raw edges even and right sides together, sew a 21"-long binding strip to each opening edge. Trim excess binding and press the seam toward the binding.

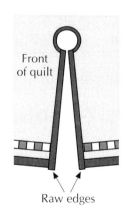

Sew 21"-long binding strips
to each side of opening
and press out.

7. Fold the binding over the edges to the back of the tree skirt and press. Fold the top and bottom first, then the center hole binding, and finally the sides and opening edges. Pin in position and hand stitch in place.

Note: The binding on all edges *except* the inner circle finishes to ½" wide. The inner-circle edges finish to ¼" wide.

8. Machine or hand quilt in-the-ditch around the checkerboard border. Quilt a 2" grid in the tree-skirt background, extending it through outer border. Outline the appliqué designs by quilting 1/16" from edges.

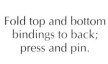

Fold top and bottom bindings to back; press and pin.

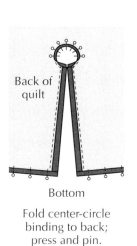

Fold center-circle binding to back; press and pin.

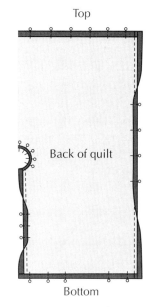

Fold sides and center-opening binding to back; press and pin.

Mr. MacGregor would surely approve of this tree skirt, appliquéd with birdhouses and bright sunflowers! ▶

Fusible Appliqué

The Christmas Garden projects require a technique called fusible appliqué. To do this, you will need to purchase a fusible web with a transfer-paper backing. Fabric stores have several different brands and types. I used heavyweight HeatnBond fusible web.

1. Read manufacturer's directions for the fusible web.
2. Trace all parts of each appliqué design onto the paper side of the fusible web.
3. Cut out around each traced shape, using a sharp paper scissors and allowing an extra margin of web beyond the drawn line.

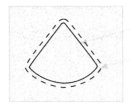

Tracing line

Cutting line

Trace shape on paper side of fusible web.
Cut out with extra margin.

4. Following manufacturer's directions, fuse each prepared shape to the *wrong side* of the selected appliqué fabric. Cut out each shape on the drawn line and remove the backing paper. A thin film of fusible web will remain on the wrong side of each piece.

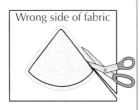

Wrong side of fabric

5. Unless otherwise instructed in the specific project directions, arrange all the pieces of each design on the background fabric. When everything is in position, fuse in place.

Position all pieces and fuse at once.

Tip: When placing appliqué pieces for the projects in this chapter, remember, they are the reverse of the pattern that was traced because you traced them onto the paper side of the fusible web. When positioned and fused, the designs will match those shown in the photos.

No-Sew Ornaments

Finished Size: Varies (See ornament templates.)

The whole family can work together to create these easy ornaments. Eleven different garden motifs include watering cans, birdhouses, sunflowers, watermelons, and ladybugs. It's easy to convert these ornament designs into personalized gift tags, too.

Materials

Several coordinated scraps or ⅛-yd. pieces of printed cottons for ornaments
Heavyweight, paper-backed fusible web, such as HeatnBond
1 button, ½" to ⅝" diameter, for each watering can ornament
4 black buttons, each ⅛" diameter, for each ladybug ornament
1 package each of natural and green raffia for hangers
Tacky craft glue

Assembly

Use the patterns on pages 78–79.
Refer to the photos on page 61.

1. Trace and prepare each appliqué shape as described for "Fusible Appliqué," at left. *Be sure to trace on the outside of the heavy line of each design.* Trace each design detail, such as the heart for the watering can, too. Trace one pattern piece for each ornament.

Trace designs and details separately.

2. Cut out each shape, leaving a little extra margin around each as shown in the directions for "Fusible Appliqué." Do not cut out ornament details yet.
3. Fuse the traced ornament pattern to the wrong side of the main ornament fabric. Cut out the ornament on the drawn line and remove the paper backing.

4. *Cut a second piece of fusible web that is slightly larger than the outer edges of the ornament shape. Leave the paper backing on these unmarked pieces of fusible web.* Fuse to the wrong side of the fabric that you want on the back side of the ornament (usually the same as the main ornament fabric). Do not remove the paper. It will stay on this fabric to add body to the finished ornament.

Tip: The paper will remain on the second piece, so if you are using HeatnBond fusible web, avoid tracing designs in areas with red lines when using light-colored fabric. The red line may show through the fabric.

5. Position the cutout ornament shape *on the paper side* of the unmarked shape and fuse.

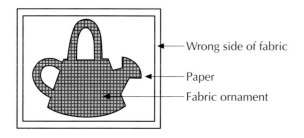

— Wrong side of fabric
— Paper
— Fabric ornament

6. Using the ornament edges as a guide, trim the second piece of fusible web to match the cut piece. Now your ornament has a finished front and back!
7. Cut the design details from the fusible web, leaving a little margin around each piece as you did for the ornament shape. Fuse the traced pieces to the wrong side of selected fabrics. Cut out the design details on the marked line, remove the paper backing, and fuse to ornament fronts. Trim outer edges if necessary.
8. Add button embellishments with tacky glue.
9. For each ornament hanger, cut an 8"- to 9"-long piece of raffia. Make a loop by knotting the ends together. Glue the knotted end of the hanger to the back side of the ornament.

No-Sew Gift Tags
Finished Size: Varies (See ornament templates.)

If you make No-Sew Ornaments as gifts, add a piece of fabric for the name of the recipient, following the simple directions below.

Materials and Tools

Paper-backed fusible web, such as HeatnBond
Scrap of light-colored or muslin fabric
Permanent fine-point felt pen
Black perle cotton or crochet thread
Pinking shears

Assembly

1. Make desired ornament(s).
2. For each tag, cut a piece of fusible web approximately 1½" x 2½". Fuse to the wrong side of a scrap of light-colored fabric or muslin. Trim the fabric even with the edges of the paper backing.
3. Remove the paper backing from the fusible web and trim the edges of the tag with pinking shears. You may have to adjust the size of the fabric piece to fit the ornament design that you have selected.
4. Position the fabric piece on the back side of the completed ornament and fuse in position.
5. Use a permanent fine-point felt pen to write the words TO: and FROM: on the tag as shown.

Tip: Write letters in pencil first, then in felt pen. If you like, add dots to the letters. It can disguise any unevenness in your printing.

To:
From:

6. To add a tie to the ornament, cut a 6"-long piece of black perle cotton or crochet thread. Thread through a sharp needle and pull through the top of each gift tag. Tie the loose ends in a knot.

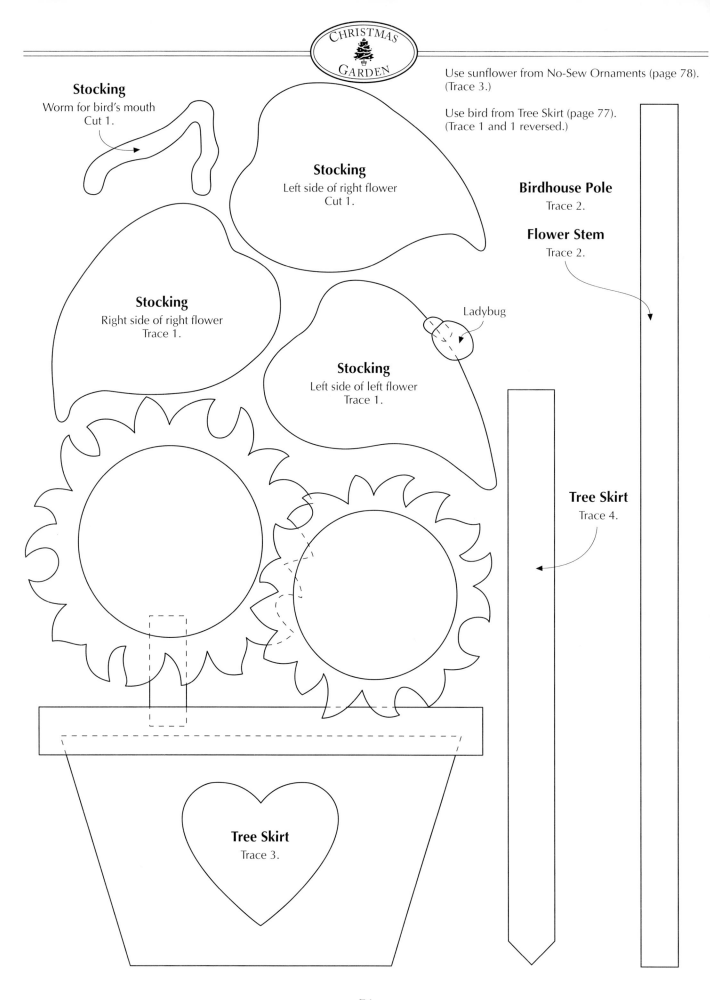

Stocking

Worm for bird's mouth
Cut 1.

Stocking

Left side of right flower
Cut 1.

Stocking

Right side of right flower
Trace 1.

Stocking

Left side of left flower
Trace 1.

Ladybug

Use sunflower from No-Sew Ornaments (page 78).
(Trace 3.)

Use bird from Tree Skirt (page 77).
(Trace 1 and 1 reversed.)

Birdhouse Pole

Trace 2.

Flower Stem

Trace 2.

Tree Skirt

Trace 4.

Tree Skirt

Trace 3.

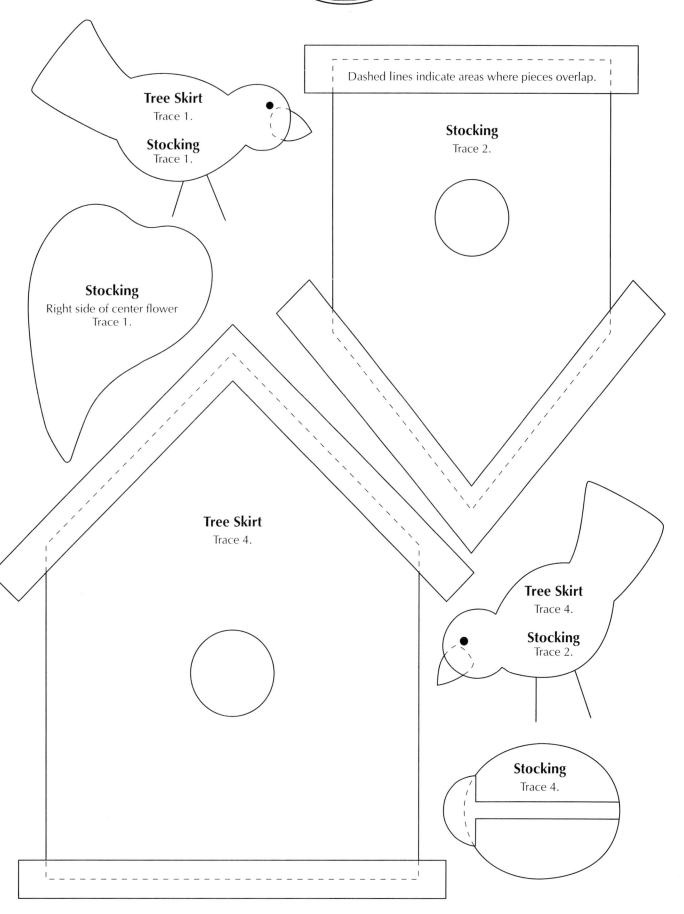

Tree Skirt
Trace 1.

Stocking
Trace 1.

Dashed lines indicate areas where pieces overlap.

Stocking
Trace 2.

Stocking
Right side of center flower
Trace 1.

Tree Skirt
Trace 4.

Tree Skirt
Trace 4.

Stocking
Trace 2.

Stocking
Trace 4.

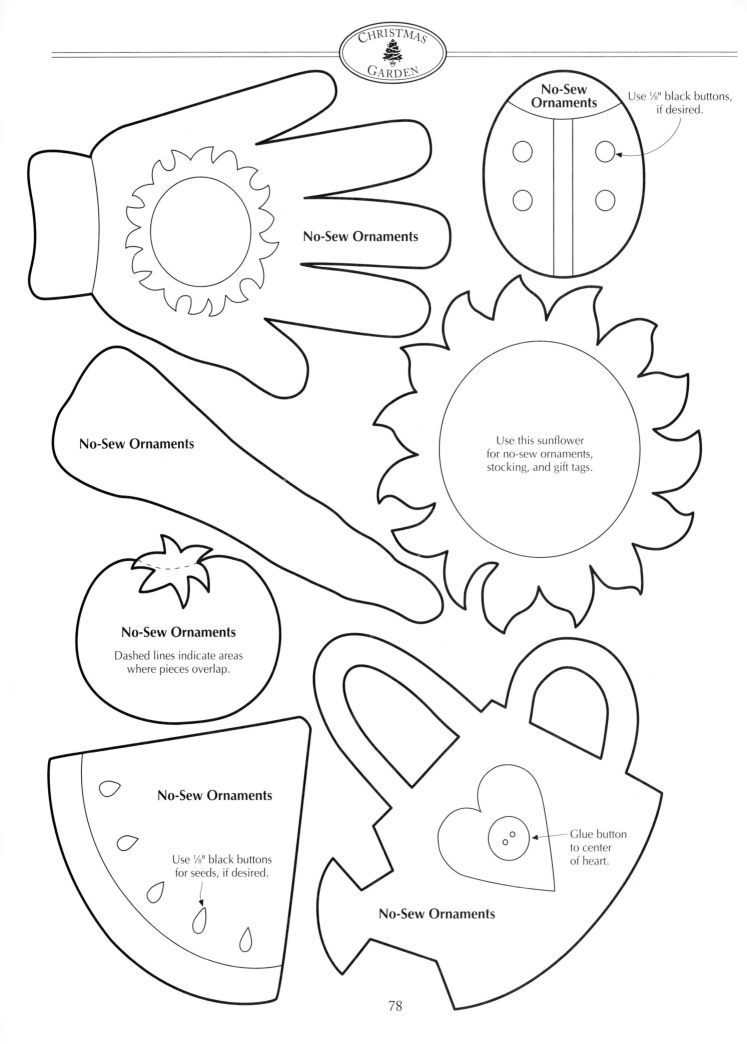

No-Sew Ornaments

No-Sew Ornaments

No-Sew Ornaments

Use ⅛" black buttons, if desired.

Use this sunflower for no-sew ornaments, stocking, and gift tags.

No-Sew Ornaments

No-Sew Ornaments

Dashed lines indicate areas where pieces overlap.

No-Sew Ornaments

Use ⅛" black buttons for seeds, if desired.

Glue button to center of heart.

No-Sew Ornaments

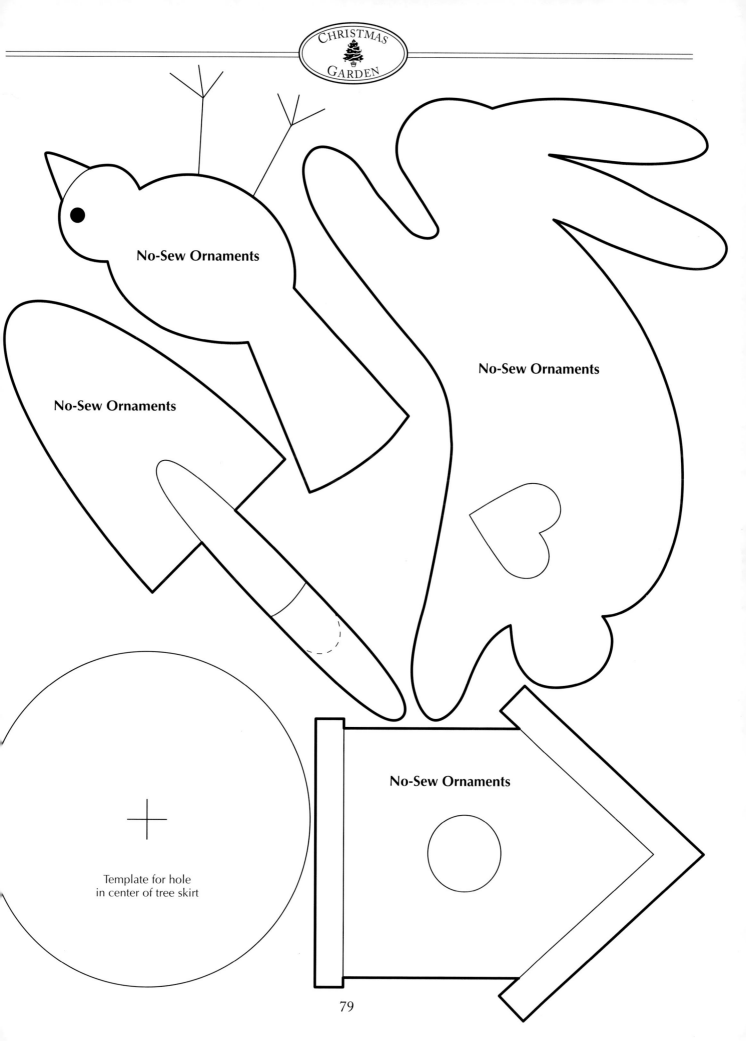

No-Sew Ornaments

No-Sew Ornaments

No-Sew Ornaments

No-Sew Ornaments

+

Template for hole
in center of tree skirt

European Opulence

by Sue Thom

◄ Fit for the Sun King's palace or a formal setting in your home, elegant topiaries and sun, moon, and star ornaments adorn this festive tree. Gilded glass ornaments, eucalyptus sprays, and bunches of gold grapes festoon the branches amid golden garlands of ribbon.

Celestial ornaments and gilded eucalyptus sprays were tied with yards of gold ribbon to crown this resplendent tree. ▶

An elegant focal point for mantel or table, this topiary is made of dried flower petals and pepper berries and trimmed with wire-edged silk ribbon. For much less than a king's ransom, inexpensive and simple sponge painting transformed plain brown kraft paper and cardboard boxes into gilded gift boxes and wrapping paper. The same technique was used to gild the glass-ball ornaments. ▼

81

*W*hen I think of Europe, my mind turns to old-world charm and history—an imaginary time of classical elegance. With that feeling in mind, I designed this Christmas tree filled with old-world style. Subtle gold glitter sparkles on natural ornaments and sprays of eucalyptus. Gilded and antiqued celestial ornaments shimmer in the branches with a mystical feeling of long-ago times. Glass balls finished with faux gold leafing represent the jewels hidden in ancient castles, just waiting to be discovered. Golden antique boxes evoke memories of those private treasures so dear to each of us, holding secrets of our past to cherish forever. Individual topiary ornaments summon thoughts of stately mansions, with finely manicured lawns and elegantly designed gardens.

While designing this mystical tree, I let my mind wander to another time and place. I hope you enjoy my European Opulence as much as I have.

Sue Thom

After studying home economics and textile design, Sue Thom wanted to share her enjoyment of sewing and crafts with others. She designed and sewed custom patchwork clothing and home accessories and sold her work through a variety of boutiques and art fairs in the Pacific Northwest. She has written four publications for That Patchwork Place and continues to teach classes on design and constructing home-decorating accessories for a quilt store in the Seattle area. Sue's European Opulence tree is a sparkling example of her creativity and eye for design.

Trim-the-Tree Shopping List

✔ Wide gold mesh ribbon to drape in the branches as a garland

✔ White mini lights

✔ Large bunches of golden grapes to tuck among the branches

✔ Plum-colored tissue paper for packages

✔ Candles, greenery, and artificial pears for the mantel

✔ Garland for the staircase

Note: Fill miniature baskets with tiny pine cones and Spanish moss and spray gold for additional ornaments. Gilded pine cones are another nice addition to the ornaments for this tree. Glue a golden cord to the top for hanging. Fill a large basket with golden pine cones for an easy centerpiece.

Hydrangea Topiaries

Finished Size: Varies with size of container

Materials

Styrofoam ball approximately the same width as the container
Design Master Color Tone* (green, blue, or purple)
7"-long twig (approximately 3 times the height of the container you are using)
2¼"-tall clay pot or other container
Floral foam
Moss
Dried flowers**
Approximately ½ yd. of wire-edged gold mesh ribbon
Fine wire
Clear spray-on craft sealer
Craft glue or glue gun and glue
Small, sharp knife

*Design Master Color Tone is a color solution that allows unlimited creativity. More like a dye than paint, you can use light multiple coats that dry in seconds. You can use it on a variety of surfaces including fresh flowers, dried natural materials, paper, fabric, and wood. Look for it at craft-supply stores. Florists sometimes carry it as well.

**Purchase flowers or dry your own, following the directions on page 84.

Assembly

See photo on page 81.

1. Spray the Styrofoam ball with green, blue, or purple Design Master Color Tone.
2. Using a sharp knife, make a point on one twig end.

3. Using craft glue or a glue gun, glue the floral foam inside the container, then glue the blunt end of the twig in the floral foam.

4. Poke the pointed end of the twig into the Styrofoam ball and add a little glue to secure. Insert wire next to the twig until 1½" extends above the top of the Stryofoam ball. Fold it over to form a loop for hanging. Wrap the bottom end of the wire loop around the twig near the ball.

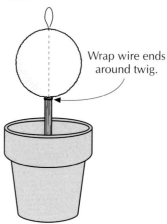

Wrap wire ends around twig.

5. Glue moss and flowers over the entire surface of the Styrofoam ball.
6. Spray flowers and twig with clear spray sealer.
7. Mound and glue moss around the top of container, covering the floral foam. Tie the wire-edged gold ribbon around the twig in a bow, covering the wire just under the ball of flowers. Cut ribbon ends at an angle.

Tip: *Make a larger topiary to use as a decorative accent on coffee table or hearth.*

Drying Hydrangeas

Use dried hydrangeas in topiaries and wreaths and as a color variation in potpourri. Tuck them randomly in the branches of the Christmas tree or wrap large bouquets of them in beautiful tissue paper and tie with gold ribbon. They're pretty enough to give as gifts to those who love dried flowers—any time of the year.

Hydrangeas are one of the easiest and most rewarding of all flowers to dry. Cut them at the end of the season, just before the first frost. If they are cut too early, they will wilt before they dry. When the flowers begin to have a leathery feel, cut a test flower with its stem and hang it upside down in a dark area. If it has not wilted by the second day, it is safe to harvest the flowers from the entire bush.

If some of the flowers have turned brown or have lost their color either before or after drying, you can restore the color by following the directions for "Tinting Dried or Fresh Flowers" on page 85.

Drying Method One

Cut flowers with stems and remove leaves. Hang upside down in a cool, dark area. I prefer to dry each stem separately so that the flowers are not crushed, but if you dry them in a bunch, wrap them with a rubber band so that the wrap remains secure; the stems will shrink during the drying process.

Drying Method Two

You will need glycerin, which is available at drugstores and farm-supply stores.

Cut flowers with stems and remove leaves. Mix 1 part glycerin with 2 parts water and boil until well mixed. Cool slightly. While the solution is still warm, pour it into a jar or vase.

Place the freshly cut hydrangeas in the solution and allow to stand for 24 hours, then hang to dry as described in Method One.

This method allows the glycerin solution to be absorbed into the stems and flowers, keeping them soft after drying. Unfortunately, this method also removes the natural color from the flowers, leaving them a tan color. You can leave them as is or tint them, following the directions for "Tinting Dried or Fresh Flowers," on page 85.

Drying Small Cut Flowers

You will need silica gel, sold at craft-supply stores. If not available, use a mixture of two parts of cornmeal to one part Borax.

Place a layer of silica gel in a low container, then place flower heads face up and cover with more silica gel. Allow to dry. The length of drying time depends on a variety of conditions, including the amount of humidity in the air, so begin checking after the second day. Drying can take from two to five days.

Tinting Dried or Fresh Flowers

Dried flowers often lose their natural coloring after drying or with age, and fresh flowers can lose their color due to weather conditions. I use a combination of Design Master Color Tone colors, available from craft-supply stores, on both fresh and dried flowers to enhance or replace their natural colors. Experiment with this technique on less-than-perfect flowers first.

Using a Design Master Color Tone held approximately 15" away from the flower, lightly mist with one color, then the next, until the desired color is achieved. To create a more natural appearance, use layers of more than one color. It is not necessary to allow the paint to dry between coats. In fact, layering while wet often helps colors blend.

I recommend using the following colors for tinting hydrangeas: burgundy, cranberry, violet, cornflower blue, Wedgwood blue, lavender, and/or dusty rose.

Gilded Glass Ornaments

A single ornament, beautifully wrapped, makes a wonderful holiday or hostess gift.

Materials and Supplies

Glass ornaments in assorted sizes (Original color is not important.)*
Floral foam
Thin twigs
Assorted colors of Design Master Color Tone or acrylic paints
Clear gloss sealer
*You can also use this process on ceramic or wooden ornaments.

Assembly

1. Remove the metal hanger and crown from each ornament.
2. Place a twig in each ornament for ease in handling, and following the directions for "Gilded Opulence" on page 87, cover the ornament with layers of color. Poke the twig in floral foam to support the ornament while drying between coats.

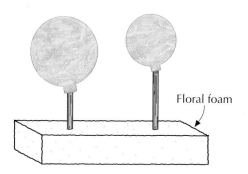

Floral foam

3. When ornaments are completely dry, spray with several coats of clear gloss sealer to achieve the desired sheen. Replace the ornament crowns and hangers.

Celestial Ornaments

Materials

Corrugated cardboard
Brown kraft paper or brown grocery bags
Craft glue or wallpaper adhesive
Design Master Color Tone and/or acrylic paints
Gold cord

Assembly

Use patterns on pullout pattern sheet #3.

Glue circle to cardboard.

1. Cut sun, circle, moon and star shapes from cardboard.
2. To create a convex surface, glue the cardboard circle to one side of the sun shape.
3. Add "Faux Gold Leaf" and "Gilded Opulence," following the directions on page 87. To create the facial features on the sun, outline them on the applied paper before applying the color. Use the point of a ball-point pen or other blunt point to do this.

4. Punch a hole in the top of each completed ornament and add a loop of gold cord for hanging.

Gilded Eucalyptus Spray

Materials

Dried eucalyptus sprays
Dried German statice or other dried natural material
Brilliant gold spray paint
Fine-gauge wire

Assembly

1. Working in a well-ventilated area, spray eucalyptus and dried statice with gold paint. Lay branches close together on newspaper while spraying to economize on paint.
2. Tie dried, painted branches together with fine wire.
3. Tuck into tree branches as desired.

Gilded Tree Topper

Materials

1 each of the Gilded Celestial ornaments (star, moon, and sun)
3 thin wooden dowels, each 10"–12" long
3–5 Gilded Eucalyptus sprays (above)
4–5 yds. of wide wire-edged gold mesh ribbon
Glue gun and glue
Florist wire

Assembly

See the photo on page 81.

1. Glue a dowel to the back of each ornament.
2. Wire ornaments and eucalyptus sprays together, arranging ornaments at varying heights with the sun uppermost. Use glue to secure if necessary.
3. Using wire-edged ribbon, make a large, multi-looped bow and wire to the ornament/eucalyptus spray.
4. Prop in the uppermost branches of the tree.

Gilded Gift Boxes and Gift Wrap

You might want to make gift cards or tags to match the gilded box or paper. Consider coordinating the colors on the gilded wrapping paper with the gift inside! Or, give sets of gilded wrapping paper and boxes as gifts.

Materials

Cardboard or wooden boxes
Solid-colored wrapping paper
Design Master Color Tone or acrylic paints*
Clear gloss sealer
Plastic wrap
Aluminum foil

*For the gilded boxes, I prefer to use acrylic paints in thick and irregular layers as this texture adds even more beauty. This does not apply to the gift wrap because it needs to remain flexible. Acrylic layers do not allow for this flexibility.

Assembly

1. Follow the directions for "Gilded Opulence" on page 87, layering colors on the box or paper until you achieve your desired color combination.
2. For the final coat *on the boxes only,* I recommend highlighting with Design Master's Brilliant Gold Spray, followed by clear gloss sealer.

Gilded Opulence

Use the following method to gild glass ornaments and figurines, wood and cardboard boxes, wrapping paper, picture frames, vine wreathes, even furniture. The possibilities are endless.

Materials

Ornament or other item to be gilded
Aluminum foil
Plastic wrap
Design Master Color Tone and/or acrylic paints*
Clear gloss sealer

*Using Design Master colors results in a thin color buildup, while using the acrylic paints creates surface texture. Either of these can be used separately or together. See list of suggested colors in "Color Combination Example," below right.

Directions

1. Put a small amount of each of the acrylic paints on a piece of foil, or spray a small amount of the Design Master colors on the foil. Working quickly, dab a crumpled piece of plastic wrap into the paint and transfer the paint to the surface of the ornament that you are coloring. Do not cover the entire surface with any one color. For color suggestions, see below. Continue this process, building up layers of several colors. Replace the plastic wrap when it becomes soggy.

Tip: I have the best success by adding many thin layers of paint rather than using just a few heavy coats. Don't be afraid to experiment with color, as an undesired color can always be dabbed away!

2. When you are pleased with the results, highlight with Brilliant Gold and finish with one or several coats of the clear gloss sealer to add sheen.

Faux Gold Leaf

Use bits of brown paper soaked in water to create the look of gold leaf on the surface of ornaments and gift boxes. Then add color, following the directions for "Gilded Opulence," at left.

Materials

Brown kraft paper or brown grocery bags
Craft glue or premixed wallpaper adhesive
Ornament, box, figurine, etc. to be gilded
Assorted acrylic paints—moss green, violet, copper, antique gold, brilliant gold
Clear gloss sealer

Directions

1. Soak brown paper in warm water until soft. Squeeze out water and tear into irregular shapes.
2. Using the craft glue or wall paper adhesive, paste paper pieces onto the shape (ornament, box, figurine) to be gilded, covering sides and edges.
3. Continue to layer paper until desired depth is achieved, making sure each layer is dry before adding another. To hasten drying time, place on racks in 200°F oven, rotating often to prevent sticking and curling.
4. When items are thoroughly dry, apply a glaze of color, following the directions and using the colors in the "Color Combination Example," below.

Color Combination Example

Begin with Moss Green and layer on additional colors in the order given: Copper, Brilliant Gold, Violet, Antique Gold, Copper, Brilliant Gold.

Naughty Kittens

by Barb Tourtillotte

Playful kittens and a bead-and-yarn garland chase stuffed mice around and around and up and down the tree. One naughty kitten is clinging to the very top. Balls of yarn are tucked into the branches, and cheerful colored mini lights make this Christmas tree bright! More kittens tangled in yarn play on the tree skirt, and a curious kitten peers from the stocking top!

Perhaps this kitten has already found his catnip treats hidden in the toe of the stocking. ▶

Colorful kittens frolic on the generously sized tree skirt. Prairie Points finish the outer edge. ▼

89

"No! Don't touch!" is heard by our little ones so often during the holiday season. Heirloom decorations and breakable ornaments are hands off, much to the dismay of the children. These brightly colored Naughty Kittens are next to indestructible and a nice way for children to celebrate Christmas. The Kitten ornaments and Beaded Yarn Garland are easy enough that children can help you make them. Since they are made with fabric and poster board, breakage is not a problem so children can even decorate their own tree—with a little help in the high spots. Of course, cat lovers, young and old, will delight in these frisky felines racing around the tree in search of the mini mice hidden in the branches. A basket of knitting, packages tied with yarn, and a stuffed cat add the finishing touches to this bright and whimsical theme.

Trim-the-Tree Shopping List

✔ Large red, green, blue, and teal green glass balls (optional)
✔ Garland of brightly colored plastic beads (from the dime store)
✔ Colored mini lights
✔ Packages tied with yarn
✔ Painted soft-sculptured cat
✔ Basket of knitting and brightly colored balls of yarn

BARB TOURTILLOTTE

"Craft projects are an obsession with me," says Barb Tourtillotte. "I'm consumed with my sewing machine and glue guns! It was great to incorporate my illustration, graphic design, and crafting background into this fun project."

Barb lives in Redmond, Washington, with her husband, Kirk, and three children. She has worked as a graphic designer and illustrator for fourteen years, with her primary focus being materials for the children's and preschool teachers' markets. To date, Barb has illustrated thirty published books and often uses her children as models for her illustrations.

Kittens with Beaded Yarn Garland

Finished Size: 5" x 7"

Make these cute kittens to prop in the tree branches and a beaded yarn garland to drape along their path.

Materials

⅜ yd. each of 8 bright solid-colored 44"-wide fabrics
3 sheets of 22" x 28" poster board
4 yds. of paper-backed fusible web, such as Wonder-Under
Fine-tip permanent black pen (I like Itoya brand as it doesn't bleed.)
1 skein of yellow yarn
Large bag of colorful wooden beads

Assembly

Use the pattern on page 99.

Kittens

1. From each of the 8 fabrics, cut 10 pieces, each 5½" x 10". You should have a total of 80 rectangles. Cut 40 pieces of poster board, each 5½" x 7½".

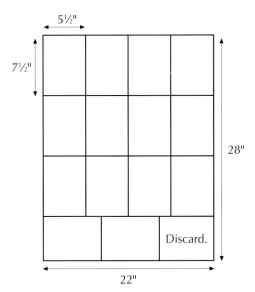

Cut 14 rectangles from each of 2 boards and 12 from the third board.

2. Following manufacturer's directions, apply the fusible web to the wrong side of each fabric rectangle.
3. Trace the kitten stripes onto the paper side of the fusible web at one end of each rectangle and cut the strip of stripes away. Set aside. The remaining piece of fabric should be 5½" x 7½". If it is larger, trim it to match the poster-board rectangles.

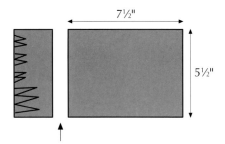

Cut away stripes here.

4. Remove the backing paper from the fabric rectangles and, following the manufacturer's directions, fuse one to each side of each poster-board rectangle.
5. Make a plastic or cardboard template of the kitten shape (page 99) and trace around it on one side of each piece of fabric-covered board. Use a sharp pencil to trace.

6. Using paper scissors, carefully cut out each kitten just inside the drawn line.
7. Cut stripes from the strips set aside earlier. Remove the paper backing from the stripes and fuse to a contrasting-color kitten, referring to the kitten pattern for placement. Repeat on other side. Trim the stripes even with the kitten shape if needed.
8. Draw in kitten faces with the fine-tip pen, referring to the pattern for shapes.

Yarn and Bead Garlands

1. Cut 2 lengths of yarn, each 12 yards long. For each garland, begin by tying a knot 8" from the end of the yarn. Thread a wooden bead onto the yarn and tie a knot to secure it. Tie a knot 2" from the previous knot, thread a bead, and tie another knot.
2. Repeat with a third bead. Measure another 8" and add 3 beads in the same way. Continue to the end.

Tip: *You may begin and end each garland with a knot-bead-knot combination if you wish.*

Create the kittens, as well as this tree topper, using a quick no–sew technique. ▼

Kitten Tree Topper
Finished Size: 6" x 12"

Materials

2 pieces of gold felt, each 9" x 12"
Scraps of contrasting fabric for stripes
2 pieces of paper-backed fusible web, such as Wonder-Under, each 9" x 12"
9" x 12" piece of poster board
Fine-tip permanent black pen (I like Itoya brand as it doesn't bleed.)

Assembly

Use the pattern on pullout pattern sheet #2.

1. Following manufacturer's directions, apply fusible web to the wrong side of each piece of gold felt. Allow to cool, then remove the backing from each one and fuse 1 piece to the right side of the poster board and 1 to the wrong side.
2. Trace the kitten shape onto the felt on one side of the poster board and cut out just inside the drawn lines.
3. Apply fusible web to the wrong side of the contrasting fabric for stripes. Allow to cool. Trace 2 sets of stripes, one a reverse image of the pattern, onto the paper side of the fusible web. Cut out stripes. Remove the paper backing and fuse the stripes to both sides of the kitten, referring to the pattern for placement. Trim even with the edges of the kitten if necessary. Draw faces with a fine-tip pen. Cut out triangle using an X-Acto knife.

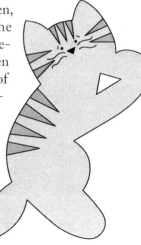

Little Mousie Toys

Finished Size: 2" x 3½"

Materials for 20 mice

5 pieces of red felt, each 9" x 12"
Gold felt scraps for ears
Polyester fiberfill for stuffing
Blue yarn for tails
Black seed beads for eyes
X-acto® knife

Assembly

Use the pattern on page 99.

1. Cut 20 mice from red felt and 40 ears from gold felt.
2. Fold the mouse piece in half with right sides together and stitch from the nose to the dot, using a ¼"-wide seam allowance. Trim and turn right side out. Repeat with the remaining pieces to make a total of 20 mice.

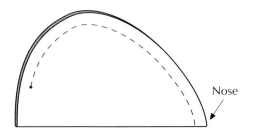

Nose

3. Stuff mice with fiberfill, turn in the raw edges, and slipstitch the opening closed, catching a 6"-long piece of blue yarn for the tail in the stitching.

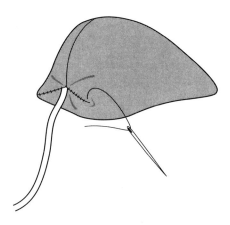

4. Using an X-acto knife, cut 2 slits, each ¼" long, for ear pieces in the location given on the pattern. Poke the ear stems into each slit. Sew bead eyes in place.

Slit

Tip: Place mice on the tree branches or add a loop of yarn to the back for hanging.

Yarn Balls

Finished Size: Approximately 3" diameter

Materials for 6 ornaments

3 skeins of brightly colored yarn
6 Styrofoam balls, each 2½" in diameter

Assembly

1. Wrap ½ of each skein of yarn around a Styrofoam ball, covering ball completely and leaving a yarn tail.
2. Nestle the yarn balls in tree limbs and drape the yarn ends over branches. Make more ornaments as desired.

Curious Kitten Stocking

Finished Size: 12" x 18"

Materials: 44"-wide solid-colored fabrics

½ yd. purple for lining and stocking pieces
½ yd. fuchsia for stocking front and back
¼ yd. turquoise for stocking pieces
⅛ yd. teal for Prairie Points
⅛ yd. gold for kitten
Scraps of paper-backed fusible web, such as Wonder-Under
Fine-tip permanent black pen
Black embroidery thread
19" x 25" piece of batting

Assembly

Use the patterns on pages 100–101 and on pullout pattern sheet #3.

Kitten

1. Cut pieces from the appropriate fabrics as listed on the pattern pieces. To cut the stripes, first apply fusible web to the wrong side of a turquoise fabric scrap. Then trace stripes onto fabric and cut out.
2. Following manufacturer's directions, apply fusible web to the wrong side of the triangles and kitten stripes.
3. Fuse kitten stripes to the kitten head, using the pattern as a placement guide. Draw in the kitten face, using the fine-tip pen. Using 2 strands of black embroidery floss, take a stitch through the face for each set of whiskers. Knot both ends near face to secure.

4. Place the kitten face against the right side of the kitten head backing. Place batting head underneath these 2 layers with raw edges even. Stitch ¼" from the raw edges, leaving the bottom edge open for turning. Trim seam and clip curves. Zigzag bottom raw edges together. Turn and press.

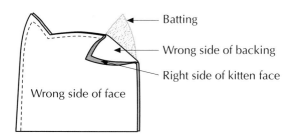

Batting
Wrong side of backing
Right side of kitten face
Wrong side of face

5. With front and back paw pieces right sides together, add a batting paw to the bottom of the layers. Stitch all the way around, using a ¼"-wide seam. Carefully make a slit in back of each paw for turning. Trim seams, clip curves, and turn right side out. Press. Topstitch "toes" as shown on pattern piece. Set kitten aside.

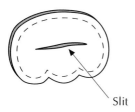

Slit

Stocking

1. For Prairie Points, fold each teal square in half diagonally, wrong sides together. Fold again to make a smaller triangle. Press.

Fold   Fold

2. Assemble 5 Prairie Points in a set for the top edge of the stocking, 4 for the toe and 5 for the heel. To make each set, insert the corner of each point inside the

other so that they measure ½" from point to point along the raw edges. Pin, then stitch ⅛" from the raw edges. Set the point sets aside.

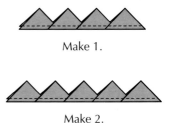

Make 1.

Make 2.

3. Fuse small triangles (I) to the fuchsia stocking base (A), referring to the pattern piece for placement.

4. With right sides together, stitch the heel band (G) to the heel (C). Press the seam toward the heel band.

5. With right sides together, stitch the heel Prairie Points to the heel band.

6. With right sides together, stitch the heel section to fuchsia stocking base (A). Press seam toward heel.

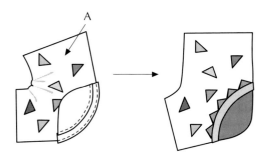

7. With right sides together, stitch toe (D) to toe band (F). Press seam toward toe. Add Prairie Points to the raw edge of the toe band.

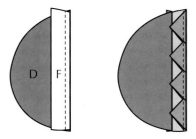

8. With right sides together, stitch the toe section to the fuchsia stocking base (A). Press seam toward toe.

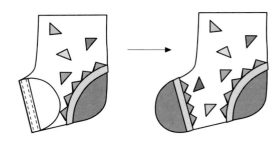

9. With right sides together, stitch the top band (B) to the top edge of the inner band (E). Press seam allowances in one direction. Add the remaining set of Prairie Points to the bottom edge of the inner band. Press the seam toward the band. With right sides together, sew the completed band section to the top edge of the stocking base (A). Press the seam toward the inner band.

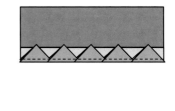

10. Turn under and press ¼" on each long edge of the loop, then fold in half and edgestitch. Fold the completed loop in half and baste in position at the top edge of the front stocking.

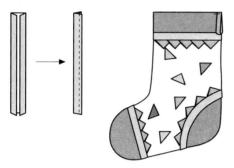

11. With right sides together, center and baste the kitten head to the top edge of the front stocking along the line indicated on the pattern piece. There will be several inches of excess fabric extending above the stitching line. *Do not cut off excess fabric* as it stabilizes the kitten's head and keeps it upright.

Finishing

1. With right sides together, stitch the completed front stocking to the fuchsia stocking, leaving the top edge open. Trim the seam and clip curves. Turn right side out and press.

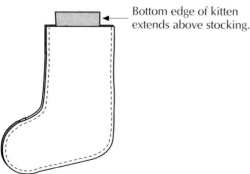

Bottom edge of kitten extends above stocking.

2. Baste the batting to the wrong side of each stocking lining piece. With right sides together, stitch the front to the back lining, leaving the top open as for the stocking. Trim seam and clip curves. Do not turn the lining stocking right side out.

3. Slip the stocking into the lining with right sides together. Stitch together around the top edge, leaving a 3"-long opening in the back for turning. Trim the seam, turn stocking right side out, and press. Slipstitch the opening closed.

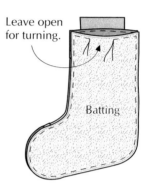

Leave open for turning.

Batting

4. Glue or hand sew the kitten paws in position on the completed stocking.

Finished stocking

Naughty Kitten Tree Skirt

Finished Size: 55" diameter

Materials

55" x 55" piece of white fabric for top*
55" x 55" piece of white fabric for backing*
5 pieces, each a different bright color and each 12" x 16", for the kittens
Contrasting scraps of fabric for kitten stripes
Scraps of brightly colored fabric for triangles
1¾ yds. of paper-backed fusible web, such as Wonder-Under
3 packages of ⅞"-wide purple bias tape
⅝ yd. fuchsia fabric for Prairie Points
55" x 55" piece of batting
1 skein of fuchsia yarn
½" dot or square of hook and loop fastener, such as Velcro™
Fabric marking pen
Fine-tip permanent black pen

*Buy extra-wide fabric in the decorating-fabrics department or piece as necessary.

Assembly

Use patterns on pullout pattern sheet #4.

1. Fold skirt-top fabric in quarters.
2. To mark the outer cutting line, tie one end of a string to a fabric marking pen. Insert a thumbtack through the string 26" from the pen. Push the tack into the fabric and mark ¼ of a circle.
3. To mark the inner cutting line, repeat step 2, inserting the thumbtack through the string 2" from the pen.

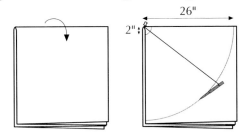

4. Cut through all layers of the fabric along the cutting lines. Cut along one of the fold lines for the opening.
5. Using the patterns, trace kittens, stripes, and triangles onto the right side of each bright fabric rectangle.

Using the fine-tip pen, draw in the legs and tail of the sleeping kitten as shown on the pattern. Following manufacturer's directions, apply fusible web to the wrong side of each rectangle. Cut out stripes and fuse to kittens, following the patterns for placement. Cut out each kitten and the triangles. Draw the kitten faces with the fine-tip pen.

6. Arrange the kittens and triangles around the tree skirt and fuse in place.

7. Open out the folds in the bias tape and with right sides together, stitch the 2 pieces (packages) of bias tape together as shown.

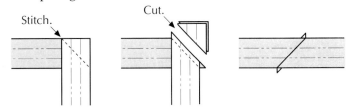

8. With right sides together, stitch bias tape to the opening edges of the tree skirt, stitching in the fold of the tape, and trimming even with outer edge. Press seam toward tape.

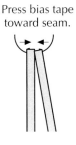

Sew bias tape to opening edges.

9. Stitch the tape to the outer edge of the tree skirt, including across the tape ends at the bottom opening edges. Press the seam toward the tape.

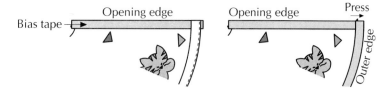

10. For the Prairie Points, cut 141 fuchsia squares, each 2¼" x 2¼". Following the directions given for the stocking points on pages 94–96, make points. Make 2 sets of 15 points each (1 set for each opening edge) and 1 set of 111 points for the outer edge of the skirt.

11. With right sides together, baste the points to the opening edges, then to the outer edge.

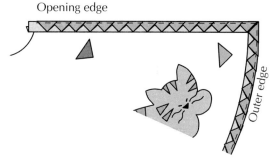

12. Spread the backing fabric on a flat surface, right side up, and smooth the skirt front on top with the right side against the backing. Pin securely. Cut out the backing but do not remove the pins. Place the pinned skirt layers on top of the batting and use as a pattern to cut out the batting. Pin the layers together and stitch around the opening and outer edges, leaving the inner circle edges unstitched. Turn right side out and press.

13. Bind the raw edges of inner circle with bias tape, turning in the ends at the opening edges.

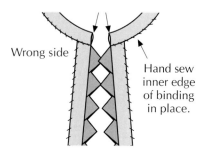

14. Quilt ⅛" from the outer edges of the kittens.

15. Lay the skirt flat and drape the yarn around the skirt and kittens. When pleased with the look, begin by securing the end of the yarn to the backing and then tacking the yarn in place every few inches with matching thread. Secure the other end of the yarn to the backing. If you wish, you may zigzag over the yarn with matching or contrasting thread to hold it in place.

16. Hand sew the hook and loop fastener to the top edge of the opening.

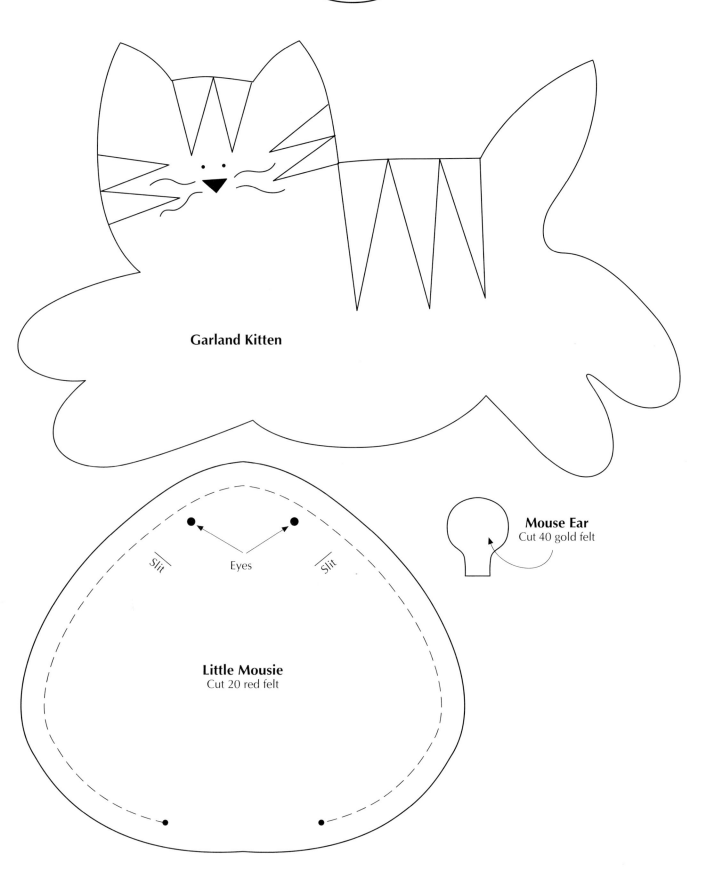

Garland Kitten

Eyes

Slit   Slit

Little Mousie
Cut 20 red felt

Mouse Ear
Cut 40 gold felt

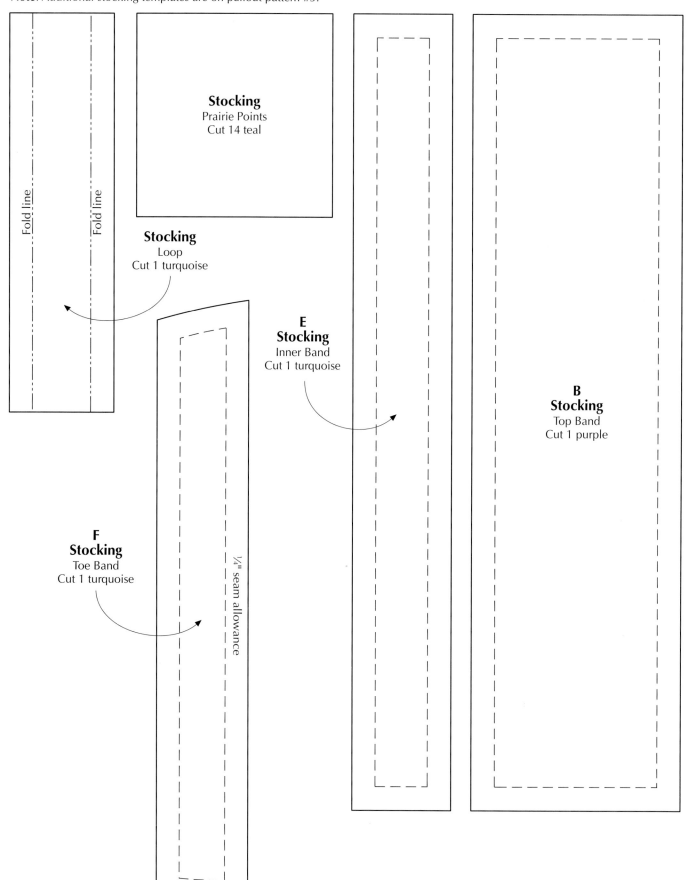

Note: Additional stocking templates are on pullout pattern #3.

Fold line

Fold line

Stocking
Prairie Points
Cut 14 teal

Stocking
Loop
Cut 1 turquoise

E
Stocking
Inner Band
Cut 1 turquoise

B
Stocking
Top Band
Cut 1 purple

F
Stocking
Toe Band
Cut 1 turquoise

¼" seam allowance

Stocking
Stripes
Cut 3 turquoise
Cut 3 fusible web

Stocking
Paw
Cut 4 gold
Cut 2 batting

Stocking
Cat Head
Cut 2 gold
Cut 1 fleece

G
Stocking
Heel Band
Cut 1 turquoise

I
Stocking
Cut 2 blue
Cut 2 purple
Cut 2 gold
Cut 6 fusible web

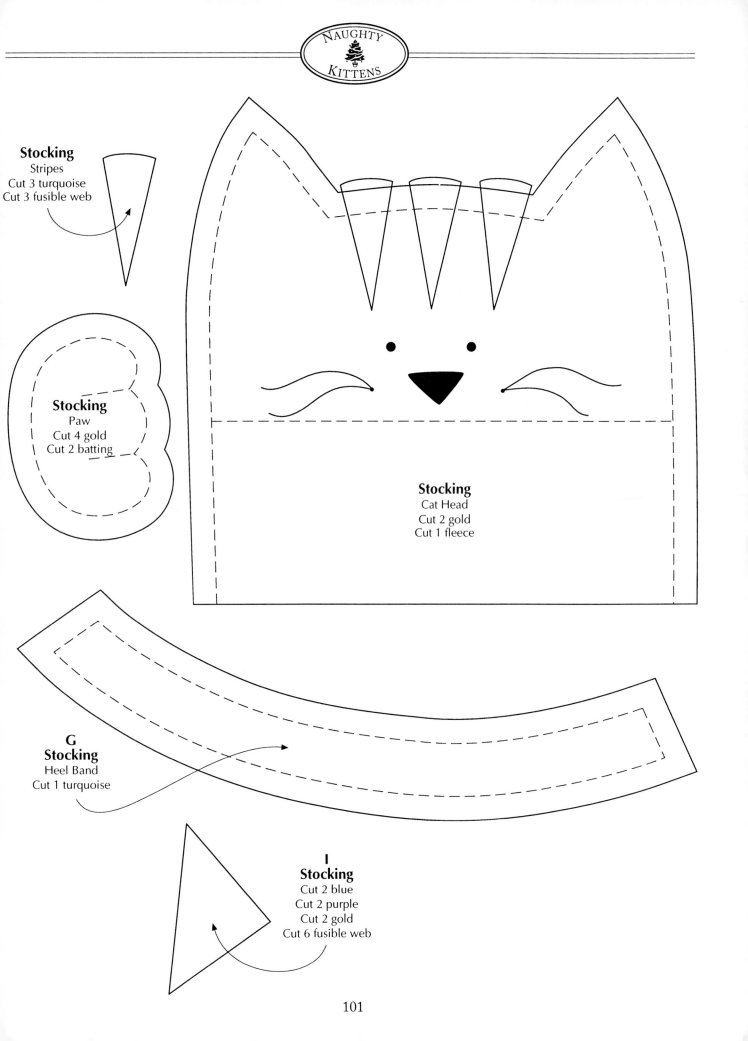

Glitzy Angels
and Bells
by Susie Robbins

◄ Irresistible, pink iridescent angels perch on the branches of this frosted sugarplum tree. Opalescent glass ornaments glow next to dazzling bells and light catchers.

▲ *Large angels embellished with tinsel hang snowflakes on the tree branches.*

◄ *Glittery clusters of metallic papers and trims decorate the tops of large jingle bells. Light catchers perch on the tree branches. Small angels hang star garlands on the tree.*

Imaginative clusters of shiny bows and trims echo the pastel colors of the glass-ball ornaments and add twinkle to the tree. ▼

I designed this tree to shimmer and shine, using lots of glitzy handmade angels, bells, and light catchers and accenting it with a collection of ready-made glass ornaments. Start with a tree that has lots of room for hanging ornaments. I prefer a noble fir with heavy flocking on the tips, lighter flocking toward the center of the branches, and almost no flocking near the tree trunk. This creates a feeling of depth to help set off the ornaments.

Plan a color scheme that reflects your taste and will look wonderful in your favorite spot for a tree. You will need bells, craft ribbon in iridescent and pastel colors, glass ornaments on wires, shredded Mylar in several different colors, and two iridescent garlands to cut up for trimming your angels, bells, and light catchers. Anything goes—as long it goes with "shiny!"

Strive for the optimum in glitz. Whatever you do, don't skimp on lights. Use lots and lots of tiny white lights. On the two bottom rows of branches, poke the lights up through the flocking to hide the wires. Work in the reverse on the upper branches, poking the lights down. You won't be sorry if you spend a little extra time getting the lights just right!

As you hang the ready-made glass ornaments in your collection, try to spread the color and size evenly, reserving the most prominent and open spaces in the tree for your handmade angels, bells, and light catchers. If you would like to add garlands to your tree, drape it with purchased iridescent and/or pearl garlands. (They were not used on the tree in the photo.)

The handmade ornaments on this tree require rather large, open spaces to hang freely. Don't be surprised if you need to trim away some branches to make room for the bells. The light catchers have flat bottoms so they will snuggle into the "snow."

Next, scatter the angels over the tree, using small ones toward the top and large ones at the bottom. For the best exposure, hang each one close to a light. Last but not least, you can use two or more light catchers together as a tree topper.

SUSIE ROBBINS

Susie Robbins is the exuberant designer of wonderful doll patterns that she markets through her company, Peddlers of Danville. Fancy, the angel on her Glitzy Angels and Bells tree, is a good example of her lighthearted approach to her work.

Susie has two trees in her home at Christmastime. The one in her family room is full of handmade ornaments that she and her family have collected over the past twenty-six years. Susie says, "Trees like this don't happen overnight. They take time to nurture." The tree she shares in this book is "her tree," which is placed in a corner of the living room so that its reflection shows in the marble entry and can be seen from the family room.

Holiday Bells

Finished Size: Approximately 9" in diameter

These bells require lots of glitz and a little gluing. Simple to construct, each bell you create will turn you on to new ideas and textures. Have on hand lots of "stuff" to embellish the bells—metallic ribbons, wire stars, shredded Mylar, glitter—you name it. Craft paper ribbons, wire-edged ribbons, and printed or plain grosgrain ribbon are appropriate choices for the bows.

Imagine using some of these bells, massed on a platter or in a bowl for an eye-catching holiday centerpiece. Or, try grouping candlesticks and perch the bells on top. They would also make nice take-home favors from a holiday luncheon. Or, how about using them as "Kissing Bells" with mistletoe?

Get the kids to help, if you like, but, for safety's sake, don't let them handle the glue gun. You'll have so much fun making these, I know you won't be able to make just one—and each one will be a little different. Have fun!

Materials for 1 ornament

3"-diameter bell
18"- to 24"-long piece of ribbon or gold cord for hanging loop
Twisted metallic craft ribbon in assorted colors*
Glue gun and glue
Embellishments—Use as many of the following as your heart desires:
  Small, clear glass ornaments on wire stems
  Glass beads
  Stars on wire garlands
  Bundles of narrow ribbon bundles
  Silk flowers

*Each bell requires at least 2 large bows. Each bow requires an 18"-long piece of ribbon (approximately). You will need additional ribbon for added layers on each bell. The amount varies, depending on how much you want to add to your bell. The success of each bell depends on how freely you can let yourself go!

Assembly

Refer to the photo on page 103 for ideas as you assemble and embellish your bells.

1. Center and glue the ribbon or cord for hanging on top of the bell.
2. Cut an 18" length of craft ribbon for each of 2 large bows. Untwist the ribbon.
3. Tie 2 large bows. Use the glue gun to glue them together so they crisscross in the center.

Glue bows together.

4. Glue the crisscrossed ribbons to the top of the bell, keeping ends of hanging cord free from glue.
5. Cut several 5"- to 6"-long pieces of twisted ribbon in different colors, untwist, arrange on top of the bows, and glue in place.
6. Embellish to your heart's content, adding clusters of gold Mylar ribbon bows, a handful of shredded iridescent Mylar, small glass ornaments, or anything else that suits your sense of "fancy." It's really OK to use a heavy hand when embellishing these ornaments. Use the glue gun to attach each layer. Consider adding silk flowers or crystal snowflakes.
7. Cut 6"–8" lengths of gold Mylar stars from ready-made star garlands and wrap corkscrew style around your finger to "curl" them. Place a drop of glue on the end and poke into place where desired.

Light Catchers

To make the light catchers, follow the directions for Holiday Bells (eliminating the bell). The crisscrossed bows form the base of these ornaments, which are designed to sit on the branches. To use as a tree topper, you may need to wire them together and then wire to the tree. For a finishing touch, to make these a little different from the bells, add a few lengths of iridescent snowflakes clipped from a ready-made garland. You could add some silk flowers, such as white poinsettias misted with glitter spray, if you prefer. Embellish to your heart's content.

Fancy

Finished Size: Approximately 8" long

Fancy is a "perfect little angel," made from a simple cookie-cutter shape. You may want to make some angels face left and the others right. Instead of attaching the hanger loop to her back, attach it to her finger or to her toe for a whimsical way to hang the angel. Make two angels to dress up a simple wreath, or hang one on each side of a mirror or framed picture.

String several angels, toe to hand, for a mantel or tree garland. You could hang them from the chandelier in your entryway using invisible thread. After the holidays, they would make a wonderful addition to a child's room.

Materials for 5 ornaments

¼ yd. of 44"-wide peach or pink solid-colored fabric for doll bodies
¾ yd. of 44"-wide fabric for the dresses*
¼ yd. gold lamé, gold Crinkle Crepe, or white cotton for wings
¼ yd. of 18"-wide paper-backed fusible web, such as Wonder-Under or HeatnBond
Fine-line permanent pens for facial features
Blush or crayon
Cotton swab
Doll hair**
Polyester fiberfill for stuffing
Glue gun and glue
Optional Embellishments
　　Clear plastic snowflakes, 1" diameter
　　Assorted ribbons
　　Glitter glue
　　Metallic threads
　　Ready-made satin roses
　　Sequins; beads; feathers; small, fancy buttons

*For the dresses, I used Rosebar's Crinkle Crepe (Mylar backed with tricot knit).
**I used "Fantasy Poof" by Fleece and Unicorn for Fancy's hair. Check your craft store for other options, including roving, curly crepe, or yarn. You can also use shredded Mylar for hair, as I did for Baby Fancy.

Assembly

Use patterns on pullout pattern sheet #2.

Doll

1. Fold the body fabric in half, *right sides together*, and trace around the doll body pattern, leaving no less than ½" of space between each doll shape. Five bodies should fit across the folded width of 44"-wide fabric.

2. Cut the dolls from the fabric ¼" from the drawn line. Since you cut them out with the right sides of the fabric facing, each pair of pieces is in a ready-to-sew position.

Drawn line

Cut out shapes ¼" from drawn line.

3. Stitch around the doll on the line, leaving the top of the head open for turning and stuffing. Clip all the curves and angles.

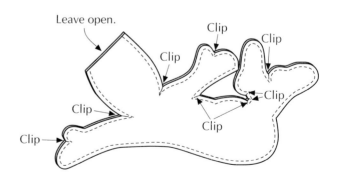

Leave open.

Clip

Clip

Clip

Clip

Clip

Clip

Clip

4. Turn right side out, starting with the toes and pushing upward with a blunt stuffing tool, such as a chopstick or wooden skewer. (Sand the point down with a nail file.) Lightly mark the stitching lines for the legs (2 locations) on the right side of each doll.

5. Stuff with polyester fiberfill. Stuff the toe marked with the * first. Then, with needle and thread, hand stitch across the leg on the marked line. Then stitch on the line that defines the legs. Finish stuffing the doll and stitch the opening closed.

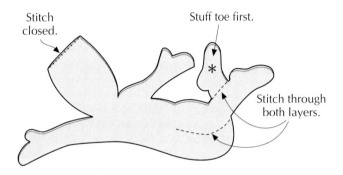

Stitch closed.

Stuff toe first.

Stitch through both layers.

Dress

1. Fold the dress fabric in half, *right sides together*, and trace around the dress pattern 5 times across the fabric. Cut out dresses on the drawn line.

2. Stitch each dress front and back together ¼" from the raw edges. Clip almost to the stitching at the neck and underarm.

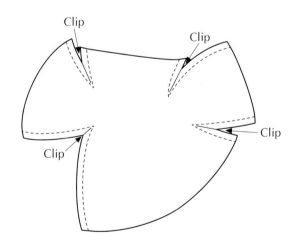

Clip

Clip

Clip

Clip

3. Turn the dress right side out and press. If using a fabric that does not ravel, pink the bottom edge of the dress to finish. For other fabric, turn under a ¼"-wide hem and topstitch with brightly colored thread. Add other trim, such as a string of pearls or sequins.

4. Turn under 1¼" around the neckline and ½" at the bottom of each sleeve.

5. Put the dress on the angel and tack in place at the neckline side seams. Gather the neckline and tack to the doll at the neckline seam lines. Repeat for each sleeve, stitching ¼" from the folded edge.

6. Add desired embellishments, gluing or stitching in place as desired.

Wings

1. Cut 2 pieces of fabric and 1 piece of fusible web, each 4" x 6", for each angel.

2. Following manufacturer's directions, apply fusible web to the wrong side of 1 piece of fabric. Allow to cool. Remove the paper backing and fuse to the wrong side of the remaining piece of fabric.

3. Trace around the wing pattern on one side of the fabric sandwich and cut out.

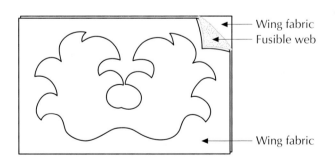

Wing fabric
Fusible web

Wing fabric

4. Use glue to attach the wings to the back of the angel's neck, then embellish as desired with snowflakes, feathers, beads, etc.

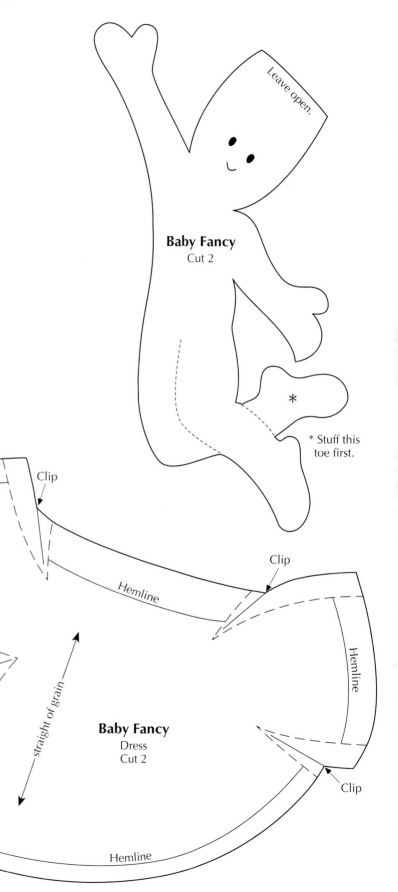

Baby Fancy
Cut 2

Leave open.

* Stuff this toe first.

Finishing

1. Using permanent fine-line marking pens, add tiny black dots for the eyes and a tiny red mouth.
2. Add a touch of color to the cheeks with a crayon or blush. Use a cotton swab to apply and use blusher sparingly. Shake excess off swab before applying to the face.
3. Stitch or glue hair to the angel's head.

Baby Fancy

Finished Size: Approximately 5" long

Use the patterns on this page and follow the directions for Fancy, beginning on page 107. Use embellishments in keeping with the scale of the tinier doll. I used pink nylon net for the dresses, but you may use other fabrics as well.

Baby Fancy
Wings
See cutting directions on page 108.

Glue

Hemline

Clip

¼" seam allowance

Clip

Hemline

Clip

straight of grain

Hemline

Baby Fancy
Dress
Cut 2

Clip

Hemline

A Stitcher's Christmas

by Kathy Gist and Karol Hervey

◀ Tis the season to celebrate stitching! Show off your love for piecing and quilting with a wall hanging, table runner, tree skirt, ornaments, and stockings. Construct a whimsical, no-sew swag for the mantel and garlands for the tree.

Purchased stockings have charming, appliquéd accents, and small evergreen trees are embellished with buttons, small spools of thread, and yo-yo flowers. ▶

▲ *A table runner made in the traditional Courthouse Steps pattern resembles colorful spools of thread.*

Quick to piece and "tied" with buttons, this tree skirt is generously sized.

As we thought about the feelings we wanted to share about Christmas when we designed this special tree dedicated to stitchers, we found that our ties to other stitchers go in many directions, backward as well as forward. When we each began quilting a number of years ago, neither of us expected it to lead anywhere special. It is one thing to appreciate quilts, and even to want to duplicate them, but it can become something altogether different as you plan, cut, and stitch. The stitches you make hold the layers of a quilt together, but they also stitch the fabric of your life to the lives of others. Although our methods are constantly changing, there is something timeless about stitching. While we sit in the present and sew for tomorrow, the threads stretch backward for generations, linking those who have chosen similar paths to express their love and caring. Whether or not we are related by blood, all of us who sew are a part of the family of stitchers.

"A Stitcher's Christmas" expresses our feelings of kinship with the generations of women who preserved and advanced the traditions we cherish. We pictured ourselves in a cabin or on a farm trying to decorate for the holidays with the materials at hand (with the help of a few modern additions too good to do without). We used old buttons, spools, and homespun fabrics to show the warmth that simple, everyday objects can bring to a room. We hope that you will enjoy these projects and use them to create your own unique "Stitcher's Christmas."

Trim-the-Tree Shopping List

- ✔ Tape-measure ribbon for garlands, or use yellow paper tape measures
- ✔ Large plaid bow with streamers for the tree topper
- ✔ Artificial green garland
- ✔ Calico and raffia wrapped packages
- ✔ Colored lights, if desired (None were used on the tree in the photo.)
- ✔ Cards of buttons, preferably old, to use as ornaments*
- ✔ Thread on wooden spools*
- ✔ Optional: Beeswax scissors (You may find these at a craft store or antique shop.)
- * Look for these at flea markets, yard and estate sales, and antique/junk shops. Don't forget to look in grandma's attic, too!

KATHY GIST AND KAROL HERVEY

Kathy Gist has been sewing and crafting since she was a child. She began quilting seriously in the mid-1980s and has taught in several quilt shops. Kathy lives in Marietta, Georgia, with her husband, Steve Sieczko, and two sons, Chip and Bill, both of whom are attending the University of Georgia.

Karol Hervey has been sewing since she was a teen and has tried many forms of crafting and needlework, but her real love is quilting. Originally from Texas, Karol also lives in Marietta, Georgia, with her husband, John, and three children, Ken, Mindy, and John Ryan.

They are both members of the East Cobb Quilter's Guild.

112

Fabric Selection Tips

All of the projects in this chapter require a variety of fabrics of light, medium, and dark values. We chose homespun plaids, stripes, and other printed fabrics that look "old." Exact amounts of fabrics are not given, except for the tree skirt, because we wanted a scrappy look. If you are buying fabrics, purchase eight to ten quarter- to half-yard pieces to use with the scraps from the tree skirt. That should be enough to make the projects as they are shown.

When working with a multi-fabric palette, choose a range of dark and light values, with heavy emphasis on mediums. Medium values play a dual role, appearing light when paired with darks or dark when placed next to lighter values. Including some lights with your darks, and darks with your lights via mediums will add visual interest. Certain colors—purple, black, brown, bubble gum pink, and a touch of yellow or gold—will give your work an older, more mellow look. Antique scrap quilts are wonderful inspiration.

The key to a successful scrap look is to avoid over-coordination. Be sure that fabrics differ in scale, value, and intensity. Don't match fabrics as if they are clothing; instead, see them as color and texture. Above all, take a few risks and have fun!

Stitcher's Scrappy Plaid Tree Skirt

Finished Size: 54" square

This easy-to-piece tree skirt is generously sized for a large tree. Without the opening for the tree trunk, it makes a wonderful tablecloth. In that case, you'll probably want to tie the layers together without the buttons, so that your dishes won't wobble!

Materials

8 different homespun-style plaids in the amounts listed in the yardage and cutting chart below*
60" square of fabric for backing (may be pieced)
60" square of batting (polyester fleece or a bonded or needle-punched batting)
Assorted buttons, ½" to 1" diameter
Black carpet thread
¾" yd. plaid for bias binding
Seam sealant, such as Fray Check™, or white fabric glue

*There will be leftovers of most of the fabrics to use in other projects.

Materials	Cutting
½ yd. Fabric A	1 square, 14" x 14"
¼ yd. Fabric B	2 pieces, each 7¼" x 14"
¼ yd. Fabric C	2 pieces, each 7¼" x 14"
½ yd. Fabric D	2 pieces, each 7¼" x 27½"
½ yd. Fabric E	2 pieces, each 7¼" x 27½"
½ yd. Fabric F	2 pieces, each 7¼" x 41"
½ yd. Fabric G	2 pieces, each 7¼" x 41"
¾ yd. Fabric H	12 pieces, each 7¼" x 7¼"

Assembly

1. Assemble the center square, following the piecing diagram below and pressing the seams in the direction of the arrows.

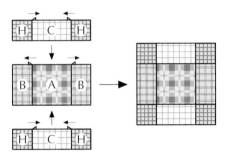

2. Expand the square as shown.

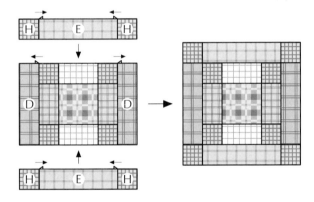

3. Expand the square once more, using the remaining pieces.

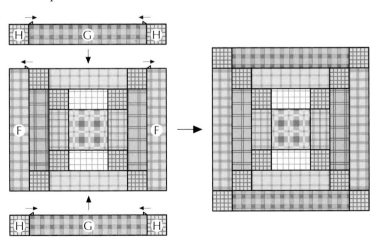

4. Place the backing square face down on a flat surface, smooth out the wrinkles, and place the batting on top. Add the completed quilt top with right side up. Baste the layers together.

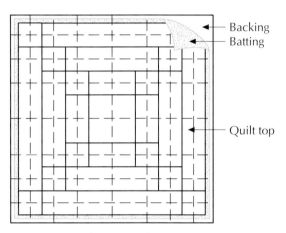

Baste layers together.

5. Referring to the diagram below, sew buttons in place with carpet thread and tie ends in a double knot, leaving short ends to show. Dab seam sealant or white glue on the knots for added security.

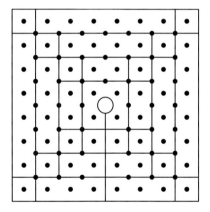

Button Placement Diagram

6. Trim the backing and batting even with the quilt top.
7. Locate the center of the square by folding it in quarters. Mark and cut a 4½"-diameter circle in the center and cut along 1 fold to create the opening.

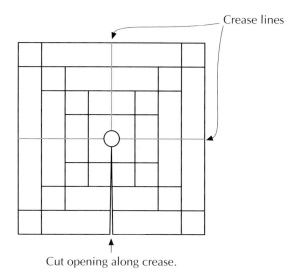

Crease lines

Cut opening along crease.

8. From the plaid for the binding, cut enough 2¾"-wide bias strips to piece a strip about 8¼ yards long (7 yards for a tablecloth). Sew the strips together into a continuous strip and press the seams open.
9. Fold under 1 end of the binding strip at a 45° angle and press. Fold the binding strip in half lengthwise and press.

10. Beginning at the folded end of the binding strip, pin the binding to 1 edge of the tree skirt (not close to a corner) and stitch in place, using a ½"-wide seam allowance. End stitching ½" from corner. Miter corners as shown. When you approach the spot where

the binding started, trim the excess, tuck the end inside the binding, and stitch.

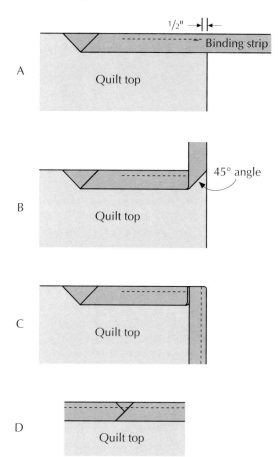

11. Turn the binding to the back of the tree skirt and slipstitch in place.

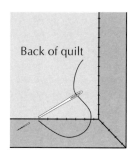

Prairie Spools Table Runner

Finished Size: 17" x 69"
20 blocks, each 6½" square,
set in 10 rows of 2 blocks each

Materials

Assorted scraps and pieces of plaid, striped, and printed cotton fabrics in light and dark shades (We used beiges, browns, and black.)

Assorted plaid scraps, at least 3" wide, for the pieced border (If you prefer, you may use only one fabric for the border; we used several.)

17½" x 69½" piece of dark print for backing

Cutting for 1 block

1. From a plaid or stripe, cut a 3½" square for the center of the block.
2. From light and dark fabrics, cut a variety of 1"-wide strips for the blocks.

Block Assembly

1. Sew a light strip to opposite sides of the center square and trim strip ends even with the edges of the square. Press seams in the direction of the arrows. Sew a dark strip to the remaining sides of the square and trim.

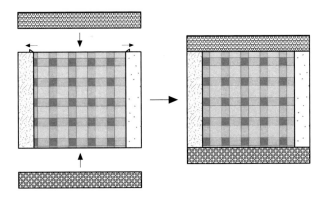

2. Repeat step 1 so that the block has 2 strips on each side of the center square.

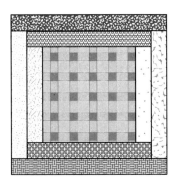

3. From the selected fabric for the last round of strips, cut a 1¼" x 24" strip. Sew to the light sides of the block, trim even with the block edges, and then sew strips to the dark sides of the block.

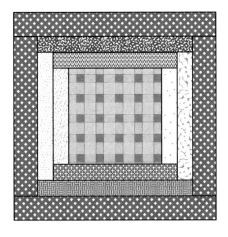

4. Make a total of 20 Prairie Spools blocks, following steps 1–3.

Runner Assembly and Finishing

1. Arrange the blocks in 10 rows of 2 blocks each, alternating the orientation of the "spool" in the blocks as shown. Sew the blocks together in pairs, pressing the joining seams in opposite directions from row to row.

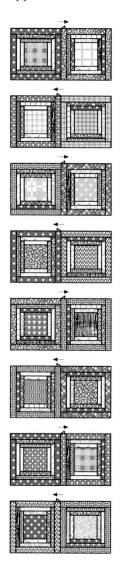

4. Sew enough strips together to fit each long side of the runner and sew in place, using a ¼"-wide seam. Add borders to the short edges to complete the runner top. Refer to the photo on page 111.
5. Place the runner and backing right sides together and stitch ¼" from the raw edges, leaving an 8"-long opening on one long side for turning.

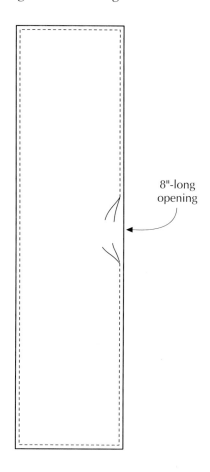

8"-long opening

6. Clip corners and turn the runner right side out. Slipstitch the opening closed and press.

2. Sew the rows together.
3. From the assorted plaid scraps for the border, cut enough 2½"-wide strips to total 180". (This includes a little extra to be safe.)

Spool Block Ornaments

Finished Size: 4" x 5"

Materials

Scraps of dark and light printed fabrics and plaids or stripes
5" x 6" piece of fabric for backing
5" x 6" piece of batting
10"-long piece of black perle cotton for hanger
Black carpet thread
2 buttons, each ½" diameter
Template plastic

Assembly

Use spool templates #1, #2, and #3 on page 129.

1. Trace spool Templates #1, #2, and #3 onto template plastic.
2. For each block, cut:
   1 Template #1 (spool body) from a plaid or stripe,
   2 Template #2 (block background) from a light fabric
   2 Template #3 (spool ends) from a dark fabric for the spool ends.
3. Make marks ¼" from each corner of the spool body at the seam intersections.
4. Sew the background pieces (Template #2) to the long sides of the spool body, beginning and ending the stitching at the ¼" marks. Press seams toward the background pieces.

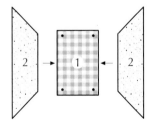

5. Add the spool ends (Template #3), beginning and ending at the ¼" marks. Press the seams toward the spool body.

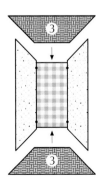

6. Sew each diagonal edge of the background piece to the matching edge of a spool end, stitching from the center to the outer edge. Press seams to one side. The finished piece should measure 3½" x 4½".

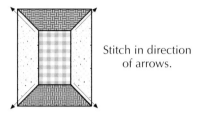

Stitch in direction of arrows.

7. From a contrasting fabric, cut a 1" x 18" strip. Stitch the strip to one long edge of the block. Press the seam toward the border, then trim the strip even with short edges of the block. Repeat on the opposite side of the block. Then sew border to the remaining edges in the same manner.

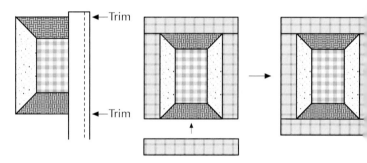

← Trim
← Trim

8. Cut a piece of fabric and a piece of batting the same size as the finished Spool block. Layer the backing and the block right sides together and place the batting on top of the block. Stitch ¼" from the raw edges, leaving a 2" opening on one long side.

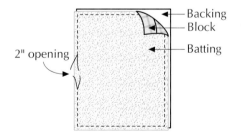

Backing
Block
Batting
2" opening

Clip corners and carefully trim the batting close to the stitching to eliminate bulk. Turn right side out through the opening. Turn in the raw edges and slipstitch closed.

9. Using carpet thread, quilt about ¼" from the seam line around the background pieces. Stitches should look primitive.

10. Thread the perle cotton through the eye of a large needle and use to sew a button to the corner of the ornament. Knot on the back. Repeat on the opposite corner, leaving 7½" of thread for the hanger and knot on the back. Add loops so some ornaments hang vertically and some horizontally.

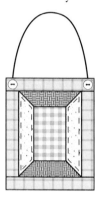

Button Basket Wall Hanging

Finished Size: 18" x 24"
12 blocks, set in 4 rows of 3 blocks each

Materials

Assorted printed, plaid, and striped fabric scraps in light, medium, and dark shades for the blocks and block borders
22" x 28" piece of dark fabric for backing
22" x 28" piece of batting
¼ yd. dark print for binding
36 buttons, each ½" to ⅝", in assorted colors
6 larger buttons, approximately 1" diameter, in assorted colors
Black carpet thread

Cutting for 1 block

Trace basket templates #1, #2, and #3
on page 129 onto template plastic.

1. **From dark fabric, cut:**
   1 Template #1 for basket bottom
   2 Template #3 for basket base
2. **From light fabric, cut:**
   1 Template #1 for basket top
3. **From medium fabric, cut:**
   2 Template #2 for block background
   2 Template #3 for block background
4. **From a different medium or dark fabric, cut:**
   1 strip, 1½" x 22", for the block border

Block Assembly

1. Sew the short side of a medium triangle (Template #3) to the short side of a dark triangle (Template #3).

◄ *Homespun button baskets add a cheery touch to the fireplace.*

2. Sew the remaining medium and dark triangles (Template #3) together, reversing the positions of the colors so that the unit is a mirror image of the first pair.

3. Sew the long side of the joined triangles to the short side of the dark triangle (Template #1), positioning the dark sides of pieced units to form basket base.

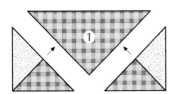

4. Sew the long sides of the medium triangles (Template #2) to the short sides of the light triangle (Template #1) to form a rectangle.

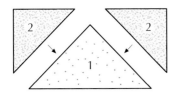

5. Join the block halves along the long edges as shown. The resulting block should be 4½" square.

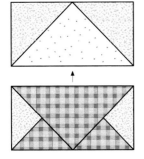

6. Using the 22"-long strip, add borders to the block in numerical order as shown in the diagrams below. Sew side 1, trim, and continue clockwise around the block.

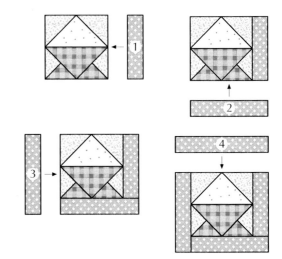

7. Repeat steps 1–6 to make 11 more blocks.

Quilt Top Assembly and Finishing

1. Arrange the completed blocks in 4 rows of 3 blocks each, as shown in the photo on page 119. Join blocks in horizontal rows, then join the rows to complete the quilt top.
2. Sandwich the batting between the backing and the quilt top and baste together with safety pins.
3. Machine quilt in-the-ditch as shown.

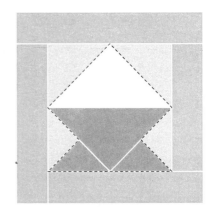

4. Stitch and tie 3 smaller buttons in a cluster at the center of each block, using black carpet thread. Sew and tie one larger button at each intersection where block corners meet. Refer to the color photograph.

5. Using carpet thread, take large quilting stitches around the basket top triangle.

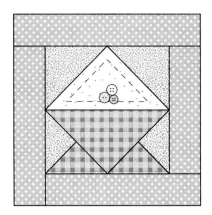

6. Trim the batting and backing even with the edge of the quilt top.
7. From the binding fabric, cut 3 strips, each 2¾" x 42". Fold each strip in half lengthwise and press.
8. With one end of the binding strip even with the top edge of the quilt and the raw edges of the binding and quilt top matching, stitch *¼" from the raw edges of the binding*. Repeat on the opposite side. Turn the binding to the wrong side over the edge of the batting and backing and slipstitch in place. The finished binding will be ½" wide.

9. Attach the binding to the remaining raw edges of the quilt top, allowing ¼" of binding to extend beyond the outer edges of the quilt. Turn the binding to the wrong side and slipstitch in place, turning in the raw ends at each edge.

Binding extends ¼"
beyond outer edge.

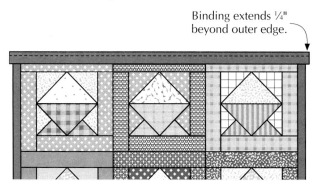

Turn in raw
end here.

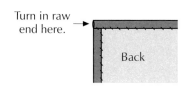

Back

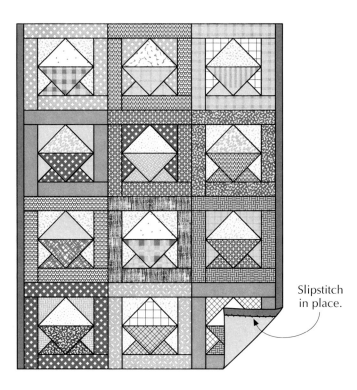

Slipstitch
in place.

Stitcher's Stockings

Embellish ready-made socks for a colorful place to hide small treasures and traditional stocking stuffers.

Materials

Tweedy outdoor-style men's socks
Assorted fabrics for appliqués
Paper-backed fusible web, such as Wonder-Under or HeatnBond
Gimp or carpet thread
Heavy perle cotton thread
Buttons

Assembly

Use the heart templates on page 131.

1. Fuse 2 layers of fabric together using fusible web. See "Fusing Fabric to Fabric" directions on page 128.
2. Cut the desired heart shapes from the fused fabric layers.
3. Position and sew shapes to each stocking, adding buttons to anchor them in place. Use gimp or carpet thread to sew the edges to the stocking with primitive straight stitches over the edges of the shapes.

4. For a hanger, use an 8"-long piece of heavy perle cotton and a large button. Attach a button as shown in the "General Directions," starting from the front of the button. On the inside of the stocking, make a knot right behind button to anchor, leaving a loop hanging free from the inside edge.

122

Stitcher's Tree Garland

The Stitcher's Garland is made of fabric hearts, hands, and scissors, cut from two layers of fabric that have been fused together with fusible web. The shapes are strung with heavy perle cotton and anchored with buttons. Make the garland as long as you like to fit your tree. It is easier to handle and store several shorter garlands than one really long one.

Materials

Assorted fabrics for hearts, hands, and scissors in desired colors
Paper-backed fusible web, such as Wonder-Under
Perle cotton thread
Buttons
Optional: Stiletto or awl if working with fabric-fused poster board (See page 128.)

Assembly

Use templates on pages 130–31.

1. Fuse 2 layers of fabric together as described in "Fusing Fabric to Fabric" on page 128. Use fabric fused to poster board for the scissors if you prefer a stiffer shape. You may use this for all pieces if desired.

2. Trace template shapes onto the prepared fabrics and cut out.

3. Thread the perle cotton through the eye of a large needle. Make a double knot in the thread end and push the needle through a hand near the fingertip. Use a stiletto or awl to start the hole in the poster-board shapes.

   Sew on a button and take the needle to the back of the finger. Allowing about 4" of thread between shapes, insert the needle near the edge of a heart from the back and sew on another button. Take thread to the back and tie off with a double knot. Make a similar knot at the other edge of the heart, sew on a button, allow 4" of thread between, and make another knot in the other edge of the heart. Repeat the procedure, sewing on a button and leaving 4" of perle cotton between, then add the matching hand. Continue to string hands, hearts, and scissors together, leaving 4" of thread between shapes and securing with buttons.

Tip: On the scissors, place the button in the center, take a stitch, and then proceed to the wrist of the hand. No knots will show behind the scissors. To keep knots from coming untied, add a dot of seam sealant or white glue.

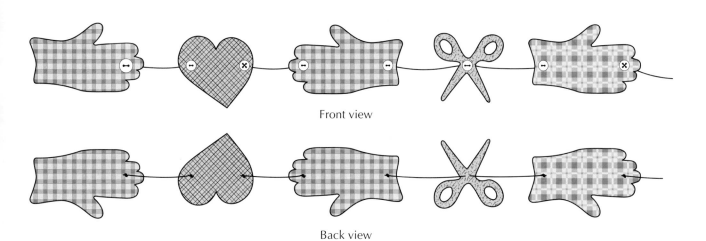

Front view

Back view

Heart-in-Hand Ornament

Materials

Assorted fabrics for hand and heart
Paper-backed fusible web, such as Wonder-Under or HeatnBond
Button
Gimp or carpet thread
Perle cotton
White glue or seam sealant, such as Fray-Check™

Assembly

Use templates on page 131.

1. Fuse 2 layers of fabric together as described in "Fusing Fabric to Fabric" on page 128. Trace and cut out the small heart (Template #5) and hand from fused layers of the desired colors.

2. Place a heart on a hand and center a button on top. Sew in place with gimp or carpet thread and tie the ends in a knot on top. Trim thread ends to about 1".

3. Using a 6" length of perle cotton and a large needle, make a hanging loop through the wrist of the hand shape and tie in a tight knot. You may wish to use a tiny drop of white glue or seam sealant to help keep the knot securely tied.

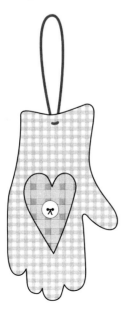

Star Ornament

Materials for 1 star

Yellow or gold fabric
Paper-backed fusible web, such as Wonder-Under or HeatnBond
Poster board
3 assorted buttons
Gimp or perle cotton
Large-eyed darning needle
White glue or seam sealant, such as Fray Check™
Stiletto or awl

Assembly

Use star templates on page 130.

1. Fuse fabric to poster board as described in "Fusing Fabric to Poster Board," on page 128.

2. Trace desired stars onto the fused fabric; cut out.

3. Following directions on page 129 for sewing buttons to shapes, attach 3 buttons, slightly overlapped or "stacked," in the center of the star.

4. To attach a hanging loop, thread gimp or perle cotton in a large-eyed darning needle. Allow about 8" of thread for each ornament. Push the needle through one of the star points from the back side of the ornament; make a short stitch on the front, pushing the needle through to the back of the ornament. By making the stitch on the front of the star and leaving the thread ends to the back, the ornament is stabilized and hangs straight.

Tie the ends of the thread in a tight double knot. If necessary, dot with seam sealant or white glue to keep the knot from coming undone.

Stitch on front of star

Mantel Swag

Finished Size: Fits an 8-foot long mantel

Materials

⅛ yd. fabric for swag base
22 old wooden spools*
Assorted fabric scraps for stars, hearts, and hands
Paper-backed fusible web, such as Wonder-Under or HeatnBond
Poster board

*These were flea-market finds. See the directions in the box below for reproducing "antique" spools if you do not have any in your personal collection or cannot find any in your favorite antique shop.

Assembly

Use templates on pages 130–31.

1. Make star, heart, and hand cutout ornaments from fused fabric layers. See "Fusing Fabric to Poster Board" below. For the swag pictured, you will need 6 stars (Template #1), 1 heart (Template #2), 3 hearts (Template #3) 2 hearts (Template #4), 12 hearts (Template #5), and 22 wooden spools of thread. Begin and end the swag with a heart.

2. Tear fabric into 4 strips, each 1" wide. Knot the ends together to create a strip approximately 162" long.
3. Tie a knot in the first strip about 1" from the end. Attach a cutout ornament to the fabric, using heavy thread and a large needle.

Tip: When adding the hearts and stars, sew them to the fabric strip through a button in the center. Leave the thread ends exposed as explained in the directions for attaching buttons on page 129.

Layer small hearts on top of large hearts if desired. Layer the heart-in-hand motifs and sew the layers together in the center with buttons, then sew to the garland fabric with a small stitch through the wrist.

4. Tie a loose knot 2½" (3" if the ornament is a large heart) from the ornament, then slide a spool onto the fabric strip, using a large doll needle, awl, skewer, or any long, slender object to poke the end of the fabric through the hole of the spool. Make another loose knot to keep the spool from slipping out of position.
5. Continue adding spools and ornaments in the same manner to complete the garland.

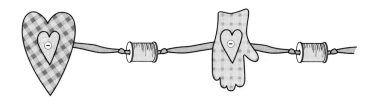

How to Age Wooden Spools

You can make "instant antiques," using the blank wooden spools found in craft stores.

1. Mix about one-half package of tan Rit dye with two quarts of hot water. Use glass or metal utensils if they will be used again for food preparation; wash and rinse them with bleach immediately afterward.
2. Place spools in the solution and stir to coat evenly. Stir frequently and check color often. Remember that the "wet" color will be darker than the "dry" color. When spools have lost their "raw" look or are a color that you like, they are ready. Let the spools dry on layers of paper towels on top of a plastic bag (to protect the surface underneath).
3. When spools are dry, apply a dot of white glue next to the edge of the rim, then carefully wind thread onto the spool to cover as smoothly and completely as possible. Put the thread end in the glue before you begin winding. With a little practice, you will wind so smoothly that one layer will completely cover the spool. Use a dot of glue to secure the end of the thread, carefully wiping away any excess.

Tabletop Tree

Finished Size: 12" tall

These miniature trees are fun to make because so many different looks are possible. If you wish, you may simply use a glue gun to attach a variety of buttons to a tree. Or, use the smallest ornament templates to make tiny shapes to hang by thread or glue to the tree. Use the reducing capability on a photocopier to down-size the larger templates for the same purpose. Make bows from torn strips of fabric to glue to the tree. Directions are given here for a spool garland, yo-yo decorations, and the square tree skirt for a 12"-tall tree.

Spool Garland for Tabletop Tree

Materials

Tan Rit dye
24 blank wooden spools, each ⅝" tall
⅝" x 60" length of fabric for the garland (See step 2, below.)
Toothpicks
Optional: Glue gun

Assembly

1. Antique the spools, following the directions in the box on page 125.

2. Cut or tear enough ⅝"-wide strips of fabric to make a strip 60" long. Tie a knot about 1½" from the end of the strip. You may need to double the knot if the spool can slip over it. Slip a spool over the unknotted end of the strip, using a toothpick if necessary to push the fabric through the hole. Tie a loose knot on the other side of the spool.

3. Leaving about 1" of space between knots, make another loose knot before slipping on the next spool. Continue adding spools in this manner to the end of the strip and tie a finishing knot. You may make 2 separate garlands or you may knot the ends together and make 1 continuous length. Arrange on the tree as desired, gluing in place with a glue gun if you wish.

Note: The holes in the spools we used were about ⅛" in diameter. If the size of the hole is different, you may need to adjust the size of the strip of fabric you use to string the spool. The holes in some spools are so small that you will need to use cording or jute instead of fabric strips.

Yo-yo Ornaments for Tabletop Tree

Finished Sizes: ¾" and 1"

Materials

Assorted fabric scraps
Quilting thread
Optional: Small bead or tiny button
Glue gun and glue

Assembly

Trace yo-yo templates on page 131 onto template plastic.

1. Using yo-yo templates #1 and #2, cut a variety of circles. How many you need will depend upon how heavily you want to decorate the tree; use about twice as many large circles as small ones.
2. Thread a needle with quilting thread and knot the end. Starting with a backstitch, do a running stitch ⅛" from the outer edge of each circle. Leave the threaded needle attached.
3. Draw up the thread firmly to gather the yo-yo, tucking the raw edges to the inside as it starts to close. After the circle is drawn tight, secure with another backstitch. Knot the thread near the backstitch and pull inside the yo-yo. Bring the needle out the side and clip thread closely so that it disappears back into the yo-yo.
4. Flatten the yo-yo so that gathers are centered on one side. If you wish, sew a small bead or a tiny button in the center of the ungathered side of the yo-yo, hiding the knot in the gathers on the back.

Wrong side

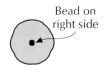
Bead on right side

5. Glue completed yo-yos to the tree with a glue gun.

Mini Tree Skirt for Tabletop Tree

Finished Size: 7" diameter

Materials

7" x 7" square of homespun-type fabric or one that will fringe easily

Assembly

1. Fold the fabric square in half, then in half again; press. Open and cut a 1¼"-diameter circle out of the center. Cut along a crease to create an opening.

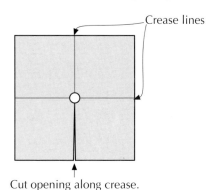

Crease lines

Cut opening along crease.

2. Stitch ½" from the outer edges of the skirt, then remove threads along edges, stopping a thread or two from the stitching to create the fringe.
3. Turn under ⅛" on the edges of the slit and around the center circle, clipping the curved edge as needed. Edgestitch by hand or machine.

How to Fuse Fabric to Fabric and Fabric to Poster Board

The ornaments in this chapter are easy to make and start with fabric fused to fabric or fabric fused to poster board (for a sturdier ornament), using a paper-backed fusible web, such as Wonder-Under or HeatnBond.

Fusing Fabric to Fabric

1. Cut two pieces of fabric of the same dimensions (slightly larger than the ornament shape).

Tip: When making ornaments assembly-line style, start with fabric pieces that are large enough to accommodate many shapes.

2. Cut a piece of heavyweight fusible web ¼" smaller all around than the fabric pieces.
3. Following manufacturer's directions, apply fusible web to the wrong side of one piece of fabric. Allow to cool and remove the backing paper.
4. Layer both pieces of fabric wrong sides together and, following manufacturer's directions, fuse from the center out on large pieces to avoid wrinkling.
5. Make desired ornaments from fused fabric layers, following the individual project directions above.

Fusing Fabric to Poster Board

1. Cut two pieces of fabric and one piece of poster board to the same dimensions (slightly larger than the ornament shape). See Tip with step 1 above.
2. Cut two pieces of heavyweight fusible web ¼" smaller all around than the fabric. Following package directions, apply fusible web to the wrong side of both pieces of fabric. Allow to cool, then remove paper backing.
3. Fuse a piece of fabric to one side of the poster board. Work from the center out if you are working with large pieces to prevent wrinkling. Repeat on other side of the poster board.
4. Make desired ornaments, following individual project directions.

Attaching Buttons

The projects in this chapter are embellished with colorful buttons "tied" on with a few stitches. Thread ends are left on to add to the primitive look.

1. Decide on button placement. Thread a large needle with gimp or carpet thread. Stitch through the hole of the button from the front, leaving several inches of thread hanging free. Come back through to the front of the button through the other hole (A).
2. Take another stitch, bringing the thread back to the top of the button. Tie the ends of the thread tightly in a double knot (B and C), applying a dot of seam sealant, such as Fray Check, or white glue to secure. Trim ends to about 1".

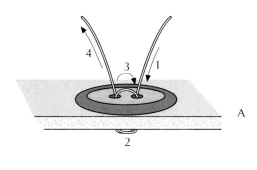

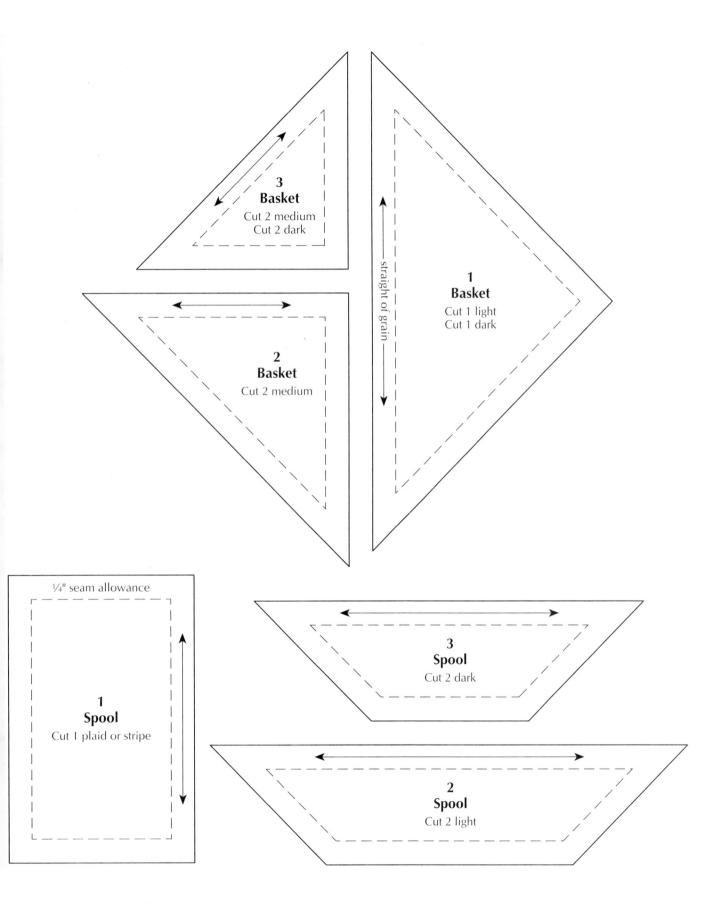

3 Basket
Cut 2 medium
Cut 2 dark

1 Basket
Cut 1 light
Cut 1 dark

straight of grain

2 Basket
Cut 2 medium

¼" seam allowance

1 Spool
Cut 1 plaid or stripe

3 Spool
Cut 2 dark

2 Spool
Cut 2 light

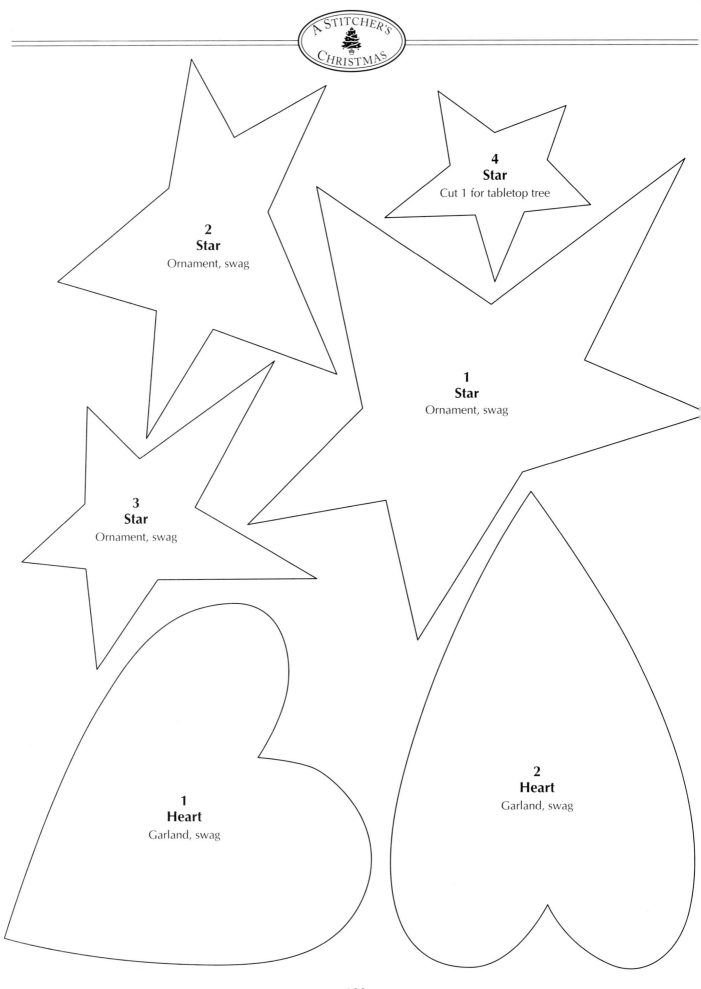

2
Star
Ornament, swag

4
Star
Cut 1 for tabletop tree

1
Star
Ornament, swag

3
Star
Ornament, swag

1
Heart
Garland, swag

2
Heart
Garland, swag

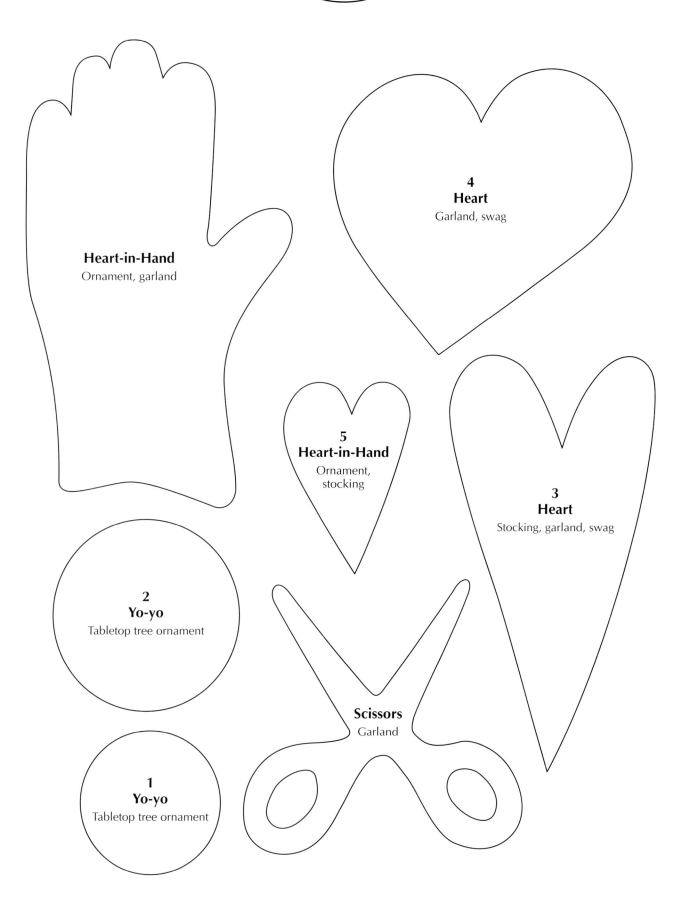

Heart-in-Hand
Ornament, garland

**4
Heart**
Garland, swag

**5
Heart-in-Hand**
Ornament,
stocking

**3
Heart**
Stocking, garland, swag

**2
Yo-yo**
Tabletop tree ornament

Scissors
Garland

**1
Yo-yo**
Tabletop tree ornament

Christmas in a Country Village

by Lynette Jensen of thimbleberries, inc.

Christmas in a country village is cheerfully represented with wonderful woolen ornaments, raffia, and bright bunches of dried flowers tied with ribbon and tucked into the branches of this tree. A quilted tree skirt, wall hanging, and Christmas stockings are pieced and appliquéd in the same warm country colors.

Machine-pieced and quilted evergreen trees, charming houses, and a white steepled church make this wall hanging one you can display long after the Christmas decorations have been stored for another year. ▶

Houses, churches, shops, evergreen trees, and stars made of wool scraps have delightful embroidered details. The tree skirt is machine pieced and quilted. ▼

Christmas in a Country Village evokes warm holiday memories of long-ago family gatherings in small villages throughout America. I used warm, rich colors and homey woolen and cotton fabrics for the ornaments, then added embroidered accents. The coordinating Country Village Tree Skirt, with its quaint houses, steepled church, towering trees, and brick-walk border is easy to piece in cotton prints and solids.

The wall quilt emphasizes the Village Square theme, one that you may wish to continue in your year-round decorating scheme. Add the generously sized Rooftop Stockings to dress the fireplace mantel. Santa surely wouldn't leave a lump of coal in stockings so charmingly pieced. Tuck small bouquets of colorful dried flowers such as tansy, strawflowers, and baby's breath in the branches. To finish this special tree, make a big bow with multiple strands of raffia tied around a cluster of dried flowers for a coordinated tree topper.

LYNETTE JENSEN

Trim-the-Tree Shopping List

✔ Electrified candles*

✔ Raffia for bows and tree topper

✔ Bouquets of dried tansy, strawflowers, and baby's breath tied with ¼"-wide double-faced satin ribbon

✔ Plaid ribbon and brown craft paper for wrapping gifts

* The lights on the tree feature strings of lights made with candles in clusters of three. Since they were very "white" against the country colors used for this tree, we toned them down by rubbing them with water-diluted raw umber and ochre acrylic paint.

Lynette Jensen is the creator of thimbleberries, inc., a distinctive collection of patterns for quilts and creative home accessories. Her business grew out of her love for the needle arts, antiques, fabrics, color, and design. Designing a tree for this book was a natural extension of her design talents.

Lynette employs six people in her small company located in Hutchinson, Minnesota. In addition, she enlists the help of others in the community who sew and quilt. She says, "The unique feature of my business is that I get to do as a business what I would choose to do for a hobby. Actually it is my passion! I am constantly surrounded by the things that excite me and give me joy, but most importantly by the people I love. My co-workers are my friends—good, loyal friends."

Lynette lives with her husband, Neil, an attorney in Hutchinson, and their two children, Matthew and Kerry.

Country Village Tree Skirt

Finished Size: 48" x 48"

Materials: 44"-wide fabric

¼ yd. Black #1 for windows, chimneys, doors, and bricks
¼ yd. Black #2 fabric for bricks only
¼ yd. total of assorted reds for House #1 and bricks
¼ yd. total of assorted reds for roofs on House #2 and bricks
¼ yd. gold for bricks
¼ yd. brown for bricks and tree trunks
¼ yd. total of assorted greens for House #2 and roofs on House #1
¼ yd. green for trees
1 yd. beige for center of tree skirt and background pieces in block
3 yds. backing fabric
1 yd. plaid fabric for bias binding
52" x 52" piece of quilt batting

Cutting

Use the templates on pages 150–51.

Refer to block illustrations below for template letters, piece numbers, and color placement. You may cut the pieces for one block at a time, assemble the block, then cut the pieces for the next. To save time, cut and stack together the pieces for each of the House blocks. Then piece all blocks at once.

1. From the background fabric, cut 1 square, 24½" x 24½", for the tree-skirt center. Use the remainder of this fabric for background pieces in the House blocks.
2. For each of the 8 House #1 blocks required, cut 1 each of Templates E, F, G, and H from the color given on the templates. Then use a rotary cutter, ruler, and cutting mat to cut the additional pieces required for each of the 8 blocks as shown in the chart below.

Fabric	Piece	No. of Pieces	Dimensions
Reds	#1	2	1½" x 3½"
	#2	4	1½" x 1½"
	#4	1	2½" x 3½"
Black #1	#3	2	1½" x 1½"

3. For each of the 4 House #2 blocks required, cut 1 each of Templates I, J, K, and K reversed. Following the chart below, rotary cut the additional pieces required for each block.

Fabric	Piece	No. of Pieces	Dimensions
Greens	#1	2	1½" x 3½"
	#2	3	1½" x 1½"
	#5	1	2½" x 3½"
Black	#3	1	1½" x 2½"
	#4	1	1½" x 1½"

4. For each of the 8 Tree blocks required, cut 1 each of Templates A and C from green, 1 each of Templates B and B reversed, and 2 Template D from the background fabric, 2 strips of background fabric, each 3" x 18", and 1 strip of brown, 1½" x 18".

Note: To strip piece and cut the tree-trunk sections for each block, follow the directions given with "Tree Blocks" on page 136.

5. From the assorted fabrics (blacks, reds, and gold) for the bricks, cut a total of 56 pieces, each 3½" x 6½". Set aside for the brick border.

Block Assembly

House #1 Blocks

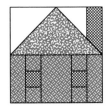

House #1 Block

1. Arrange the patches for each of 8 House #1 blocks.
2. Assemble the blocks in 2 sections as shown below, then join them to finish each block. Press seams in the direction indicated by the arrows.

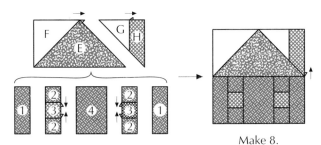

Make 8.

House #2 Blocks

House #2 Block

1. Arrange the patches for each of 4 House #2 blocks.
2. Assemble the blocks in 2 sections as shown above right, then join them to finish each block. Press the seams in the direction indicated by the arrows.

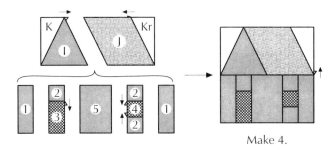

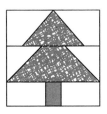

Make 4.

Tree Blocks

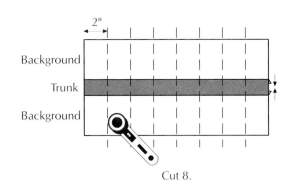

Tree Block

1. Arrange the patches cut from templates for the top of each of the 8 Tree blocks required.
2. Assemble the pieces in 2 sections, then join the sections to complete the treetop for each block. Press seams in direction indicated by arrows.

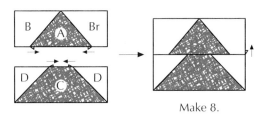

Make 8.

3. To make the bottom section for all 8 blocks, sew the background and brown strips together along one long edge and press the seams toward the brown fabric. Crosscut 8 pieces, each 2" wide, from the strip unit.

2"

Background

Trunk

Background

Cut 8.

4. Add a trunk section to the bottom of each treetop to complete 8 Tree blocks.

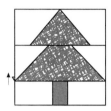

Tree-Skirt Assembly

Note: The center hole and opening slit are shown in the following diagrams to help identify the top and bottom edges. Do not cut the hole or opening until instructed to do so.

1. Join completed blocks into 2 rows as shown and sew 1 row to the top edge of the tree-skirt center and 1 to the bottom edge.

Make 1 for bottom edge.

Make 1 for top edge.

2. Join the remaining blocks into rows as shown and sew to the sides of the tree skirt.

Make 1 for left-hand border.

Make 1 for right-hand border.

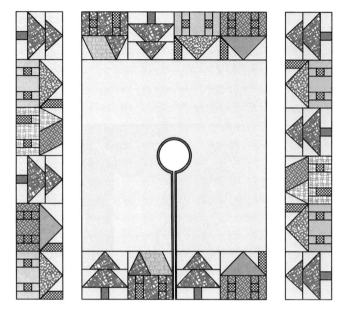

3. Make a brick strip for the top and bottom edges of the tree skirt by sewing 6 bricks of assorted colors together, end to end. Sew a completed strip to the top and bottom edges of the tree skirt.

Make 2.

4. Repeat step 3, sewing 7 bricks together. Sew to the sides of the tree skirt.
5. Repeat step 3, sewing 7 bricks together. Sew to the top and bottom edges of the tree skirt. For each remaining side, sew 8 bricks together. Sew to the sides.

Finishing

1. Piece the backing fabric to make a 52" square.
2. Layer the backing and batting and place the tree-skirt front on top of the batting, right side up. Baste layers together and quilt as desired.
3. Trim the excess backing and batting even with the tree skirt. Baste the raw edges of all 3 layers together.

4. Draw a 4¾"-diameter circle in the center of the tree skirt. Draw a straight line from the circle to the midpoint of one edge of the tree skirt. This line must go between 2 pieced blocks. Machine stitch ¼" outside the circle and ¼" away from the straight line on each side. Cut on the straight line and the circle.

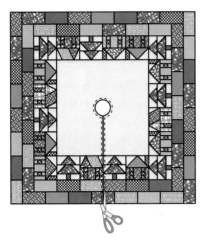

5. From the plaid binding fabric, cut enough 2¾"-wide bias strips to make 1 piece, approximately 310" long. Piece strips as shown and press the seams open.

6. Fold the bias strip in half lengthwise, wrong sides together, and press. See steps 8 and 9 on page 115.

7. With raw edges even and using a ¼"-wide seam allowance, stitch the binding to the tree skirt. Begin and end on the opening edges, mitering the corners.

8. Turn the binding to the back of the tree skirt and hand sew the folded edge in place.

9. Bind the center opening in the same way, allowing 20" of the bias to extend beyond each opening edge for ties. Sew the folded edges of the binding together along tie extensions, turning in the raw ends.

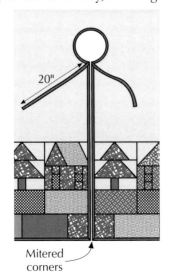

20"

Mitered corners

Country Village Wall Quilt

Finished Size: 36" x 36"

Materials: 44"-wide fabric

¾ yd. beige for center and block background
¼ yd. black for windows, chimney, doors, and bricks
¼ yd. red for House #1 and bricks
¼ yd. total of assorted reds for House #2 roof and bricks
⅛ yd. white for church
¼ yd. gold for bricks
¼ yd. brown for bricks
¼ yd. total of assorted greens for House #2 and roofs on House #1
¼ yd. green for trees
1¼ yds. backing fabric
1 yd. plaid for bias binding
40" x 40" square of quilt batting

Cutting

Use the templates on pages 150–51.

1. From the beige background fabric, cut 1 square, 12½" x 12½", for the center of the wall hanging. Set aside. Use the remaining fabric for the block backgrounds.

2. For each of the 3 House #1 blocks required, cut 1 each of Templates E, F, G, and H from the color given on the templates. Then use a rotary cutter, ruler, and cutting mat to cut the additional pieces required for each of the 3 blocks, following the cutting chart for House #1 in the directions for the tree skirt.

3. For each of the 3 House #2 blocks required, cut 1 each of Templates I, J, K, and K reversed. Rotary cut the additional pieces required for each block, following the cutting chart for Block #2 in the directions for the tree skirt.

4. For the Church block, cut 1 each of Templates K, K reversed, M, and N from the background fabric and 1 each of Templates I and L from white fabric. Cut 1 Template J from green fabric. Use a rotary cutter, ruler, and cutting mat to cut the additional pieces listed in the chart below.

Fabric	Piece	No. of Pieces	Dimensions
White	1	2	1½" x 3½"
	2	3	1½" x 1½"
	5	1	2½" x 3½"
Black	3	1	1½" x 2½"
	4	1	1½" x 1½"
Green	8	1	2" x 2"
Background	6	1	1½" x 6½"
	7	1	2" x 2"
	9	1	2" x 3½"

5. *For each of the 4 Tree blocks required, cut:*
   1 each of Templates A and C from green
   1 each of Templates B and B reversed and D and D reversed from the background fabric
   In addition, cut:
   2 strips of background fabric, each 3" x 10"
   1 strip of brown, 1½" x 10"

Note: To strip piece and cut the tree-trunk sections for each block, see step 3 on page 140 (top left).

6. From the assorted fabrics (blacks, reds, and gold) for the bricks, cut a total of 40 pieces, each 3½" x 6½". Set aside for the brick border.

Block Assembly

1. Assemble 3 House #1 blocks and 3 House #2 blocks, following the piecing diagrams given in the directions for the tree skirt on page 136.

2. Assemble the Church block in 4 sections, following the piecing diagrams below and pressing the seams in the direction of the arrows. Then join the sections to complete the block, adding background piece #6 to the top edge.

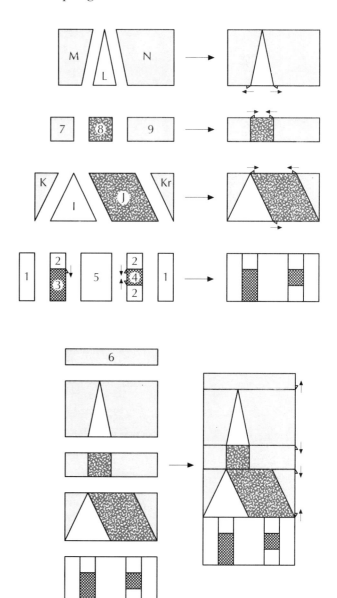

3. Assemble the treetops for the 4 Tree blocks, following the piecing diagrams given in the directions for the tree skirt on page 136. To make the bottom section for all 4 blocks, sew the background and brown strips together along one long edge and press the seams toward the brown strip. Crosscut 4 pieces, each 2" wide, from the strip unit.

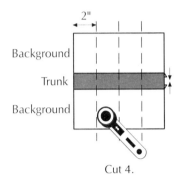

Cut 4.

4. Add a trunk section to the bottom of each treetop to complete 4 Tree blocks as shown in the tree-skirt directions.

Wall Hanging Assembly

1. Sew House blocks together in 2 strips as shown. Sew 1 to the top and 1 to the bottom edge of the background square.

2. Join trees and houses into a strip for the left-hand edge of the quilt as shown above right. Sew to the quilt top. Join the remaining trees and the church as shown and sew to the right-hand side of quilt top.

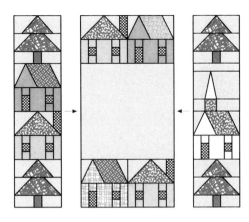

3. Make a brick strip for the top and bottom edges of the quilt top by sewing 4 bricks of assorted colors together, end to end. Sew a completed 4-brick strip to the top and bottom edges.

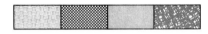

Make 2.

4. Repeat step 3, sewing 5 bricks together for each remaining side of the quilt. Sew to the sides of the quilt top.

5. Repeat step 3, sewing 5 bricks together for the top and 5 for the bottom of the quilt. For each remaining side, sew 6 bricks together. Sew to the sides.

Finishing

1. Layer the backing and batting and place the quilt top on top of the batting, right side up. Baste the layers together and quilt as desired.

2. Trim the excess backing and batting even with the quilt-top edges.

3. From the plaid binding fabric, cut enough 3"-wide bias strips to make 1 piece, approximately 160" long. Sew the strips together as shown for the tree skirt on page 137 and press the seams open.

4. Fold the bias strip in half lengthwise, wrong sides together, and press. See steps 8 and 9 on page 115.

5. With raw edges even and using a ⅜"-wide seam allowance, stitch the binding to the tree skirt. Begin on one side, away from the corner. Miter the corners. Turn the binding to the back of the quilt and hand sew in place.

Country Village Ornaments

Finished Size: Varies with ornament;
see patterns on pages 146–49.

The Country Village ornaments are made of assorted colors of wool flannel and embellished with embroidery. Use cotton scraps for the details. You will also need a supply of a paper-backed fusible web, such as Trans Web (our favorite), Wonder-Under, or HeatnBond. Follow the manufacturer's directions for fusing. Be sure to use a press cloth to avoid scorching the wool fabric.

All houses, stores, and the church require three basic shapes. You can change each one by changing the details—chimneys, windows, doors, shutters. If you want to create "Main Street" ornaments, make a variety of buildings using the basic house shape and add signs by writing the shop name on a piece of muslin to add to the ornament. Use a permanent marking pen.

The directions below include basic materials for each ornament. General directions for assembling the ornaments follow the materials list.

Materials for 1 church

1 piece of white wool, 5" x 6", for church and steeple
2 pieces of green wool, each 5" x 6", for the background behind the church
2 pieces of paper-backed fusible web, each 5" x 6"
Scraps of cotton print fabric and fusible web for details (window, doors, etc.)
Gold, black, and red embroidery floss or # 8 perle cotton

Materials for 1 house or store

1 piece of wool, 4½" x 4½", in color of your choice for the building
2 pieces of black wool, each 5" x 5", for the background behind the building
4½" square of paper-backed fusible web
5" square of paper-backed fusible web
Scraps of cotton print fabrics and fusible web for details (windows, doors, chimneys, etc.)
Red and black embroidery floss or #8 perle cotton.

Materials for 1 tree

1 piece of dark green wool, 4½" x 4½", for the tree
2 pieces of black wool, each 5" x 5", for the background behind the tree
4½" square of paper-backed fusible web
5" square of paper-backed fusible web
Light gold, red, and variegated embroidery floss or #8 perle cotton

Materials for 1 large star

1 piece of brown wool, 4½" x 4½", for the star
2 pieces of black wool, each 5" x 5", for the background behind the star
4½" square of paper-backed fusible web
5" square of paper-backed fusible web
Light gold and red embroidery floss or #8 perle cotton

Materials for 1 small star

1 piece of brown wool, 3" x 3", for the star
2 pieces of black wool, each 4" x 4", for the background behind the star
3" square of paper-backed fusible web
4" square of paper-backed fusible web
Light gold and red embroidery floss or #8 perle cotton

Assembly

Use patterns on page 146–49.

Church, House, or Store

1. Trace the building and details onto template material or paper.
2. Apply fusible web to one side of the colored wool fabric for the building.
3. Place the pattern right side down on the backing paper and trace around the outer edges. Cut out the shape and remove the backing paper.
4. Fuse the building wool to 1 piece of backing wool (green for the church and black for other buildings).

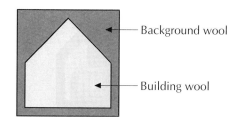

5. Apply fusible web to the wrong side of the fabric scraps for building details. Place the detail patterns right side down on the paper and trace around the outer edges. Cut out detail shapes and remove backing paper.

6. Position and fuse the details to the building.

7. Using a needle threaded with 3 strands of black floss (or 1 of perle cotton), do a blanket stitch over the edges of the details into the building fabric and over the outer edges of building into background fabric.

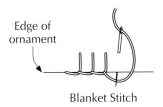

Edge of ornament

Blanket Stitch

8. Apply fusible web to the wrong side of the remaining piece of background fabric. Remove the paper and fuse to the wrong side of the assembled building to cover the back side of the stitches and add body to the completed ornament.

9. Cut out the building shape, cutting ¼" from the outer edges of the building (and chimney or steeple if being used).

Cut ¼" from outer edge of building.

10. Thread a needle with 3 strands of red embroidery floss (or 1 of perle cotton) and do a blanket stitch over the raw edges of the background.

11. To hang the ornament, add a loop of embroidery floss or perle cotton at the top.

Trees and Stars

1. Trace the tree and star pattern pieces onto template material or paper.

2. Apply fusible web to one side of the green wool square for the tree or to the brown wool square for the star.

3. Place tree or star pattern right side down on the paper side of the fusible web. Trace, cut out the shape, and remove the backing paper.

4. Fuse the wool tree or star shape to a black wool square.

5. Thread a needle with 3 strands of light gold embroidery floss (or 1 strand of perle cotton). Do a blanket stitch over the outer edges of the star or tree through the background fabric as shown at left for the buildings.

6. Thread a needle with 3 strands of variegated embroidery floss and make French knots on the tree for lights; use a straight stitch for star details.

Make French knots.

Wrap around needle 3 times.

Use straight stitch for details.

7. Apply fusible web to one side of the remaining black background square. Remove backing paper and fuse to the wrong side of the ornament.

8. Cut out the star or tree shape, cutting ¼" from the outer edges.

9. Thread a needle with 3 strands of red embroidery floss (or 1 strand of perle cotton) and do a blanket stitch over the edges of the black background shape. Add a hanging loop as shown for the buildings at left.

Country Village Rooftop Stocking

Materials: 44"-wide fabric

¾ yd. dark red for stocking front and back
½ yd. muslin for lining
½ yd. plaid for bias binding
1 yd. batting
Black embroidery floss

Note: Only small amounts of fabric are required for each of the following pieces. Check your scrap basket.

3" x 9" piece of gold or brown for stars
4" x 10" piece of white for church and steeple
6" x 6" square of green for church roof and steeple base
4" x 6" piece of red for the house
4" x 8" piece of green for house roof
2" x 4" piece of black for windows in church and house
3" x 9" piece of paper-backed fusible web

Assembly

Use the templates on pages 149–51 and the stocking and star patterns on pullout pattern sheet #1.

Pieced Stocking Front

1. Following the cutting charts below, cut the pieces and templates for 1 Church block and 1 House #1. You will be cutting pieces for partial blocks since a portion of each complete block will not fit inside the edges of the stocking shape.

Fabric	Piece # or Template	No. of Pieces	Dimension
House #1			
Dark Red	F	1	
	#5	1	3½" x 11½"
Green	E	1	
Red	#1	1	1½" x 3½"
	#2	2	1½" x 1½"
	#4	1	2½" x 3½"
Black	#3	1	1½" x 1½"
Church			
White	I	1	
	L	1	
	#1	1	1½" x 3½"
	#2	1	1½" x 1½"
	#3	1	2½" x 4½"
Green	J	1	
	#7	1	2" x 2"
Dark Red	#6	1	2" x 2"
	#8	1	2" x 3½"
	#5	1	6½" x 6½"
	K	1	
	K reversed	1	
	M	1	
	N	1	
Black	#4	1	1½" x 1½"

2. Following the piecing diagram below, assemble 1 partial House #1 block. Sew the 3½" x 11½" piece of dark red fabric to the top edge of the completed block.

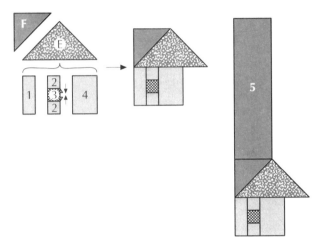

3. Following the piecing diagram below, assemble 1 partial Church block. Sew the 6½" square of dark red (#5) to the top edge of the completed block.

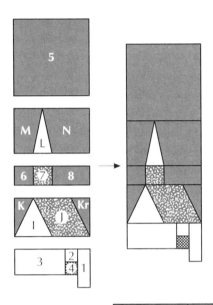

Easy-sew quilted stockings have pieced rooftops and appliquéd stars. ▼

4. Sew the church unit and the house unit together, as shown, using a ¼"-wide seam. Press seam to one side.

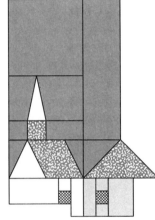

5. Position the stocking pattern over the pieced stocking front and cut out the stocking shape.

6. Following manufacturer's directions, apply fusible web to the wrong side of the star fabric.

7. Trace 3 star shapes on the paper side of the fusible web and cut out. Remove the backing paper and position stars on the pieced stocking as desired. Fuse in place, then do a blanket stitch (page 142) over the raw edges, using a needle threaded with 2 strands of black embroidery floss.

Blanket stitch stars to stockin

8. Cut a 12" x 20" piece of muslin for the lining and a 12" x 20" piece of batting. Layer the muslin, batting, and pieced stocking front and pin or baste the three layers together. Quilt as desired.

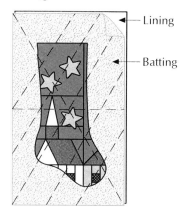

- Lining
- Batting

Baste layers together.

9. Trim the lining and batting even with the raw edge of the stocking front and baste the raw edges together.

10. From the dark red, cut a 3" x 9" piece. Fold in half lengthwise, wrong sides together, and press. With raw edges even, stitch the binding to the top edge of the pieced stocking, using a $\frac{3}{8}$"-wide seam. Then turn the binding to the muslin side of the stocking and hand stitch in place. Trim any excess binding even with the stocking edges.

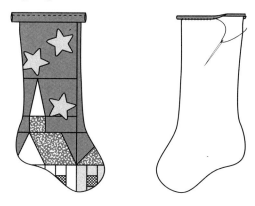

Stocking Back

1. For the stocking back, cut a 12" x 20" piece of each of the following fabrics: dark red, muslin, and batting. Also cut a 3" x 12" piece of the dark red for binding the top edge.

2. Layer the background fabric, batting, and muslin. Pin and baste the layers together across the top edge. Apply the binding to the top edge as shown for the stocking front in step 10.

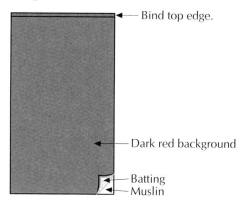

- Bind top edge.
- Dark red background
- Batting
- Muslin

Finishing

1. Place the quilted stocking front face up on top of the muslin side of the layered fabrics for the stocking back, making sure the top bound edges are even. Pin. Baste through all layers $\frac{1}{4}$" from the raw edges of the front.

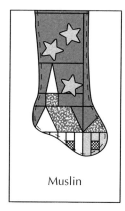

Muslin

2. Trim the stocking-back layers even with the stocking-front edges.

3. From the plaid binding fabric, cut enough 3"-wide bias strips to make 1 piece approximately 55" long. Piece the strips and press seams open as shown on page 138.

4. Fold the binding strip in half lengthwise, wrong sides together, and press.

5. Position binding with raw edges even on the right side of the stocking front at the upper right corner. Allow binding to extend ½" above the top edge. Stitch the binding to the stocking, using a ⅜"-wide seam allowance and easing it around the curves at the toe and heel. Trim the excess binding above the stocking at the left-hand edge only to 5½".

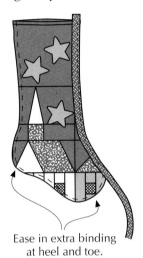

Ease in extra binding
at heel and toe.

6. Turn the binding to the back of the stocking and hand sew in place. Sew the folded edges of the binding extension together. Turn under the raw end and fold it to the back of the stocking to form a hanging loop about 2½" long. Stitch in place.

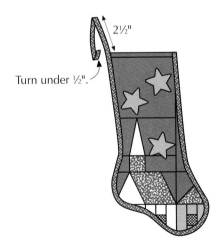

2½"

Turn under ½".

Country Village
Ornaments

Gallery

Country Village
Ornaments

Chimney Choices

Antiques

Large Star

Sweets

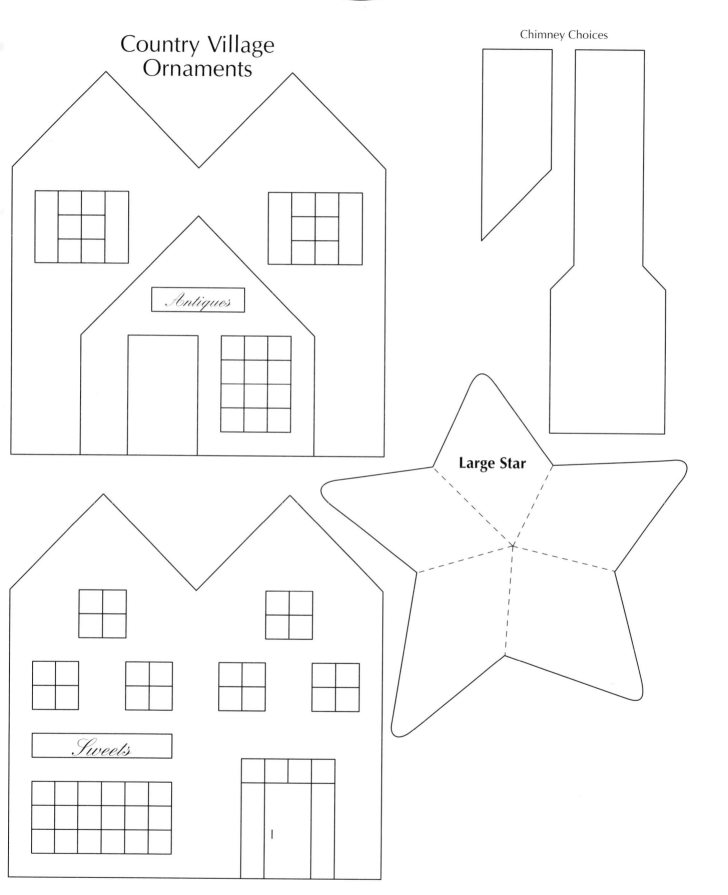

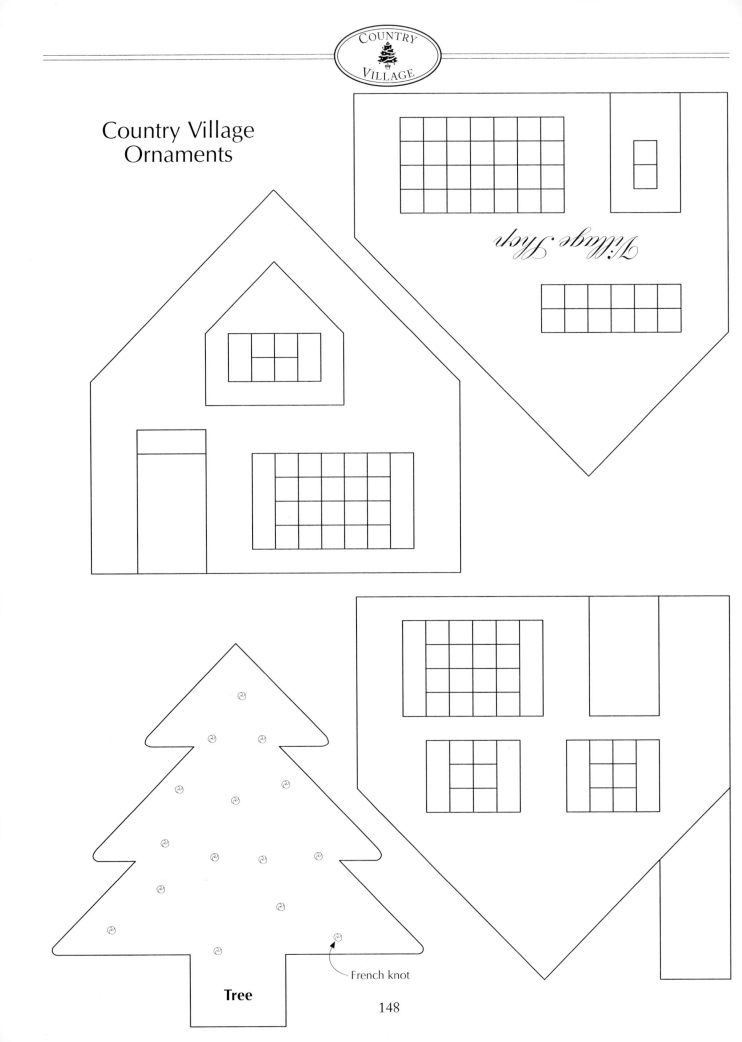

Country Village
Ornaments

Village Shop

Tree

French knot

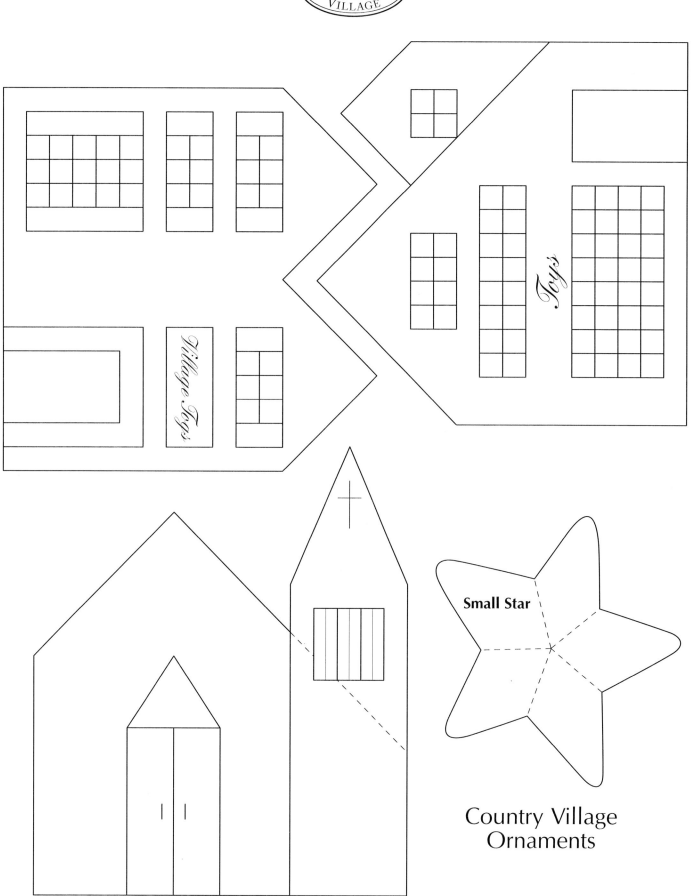

Village Toys

Toys

Small Star

Country Village
Ornaments

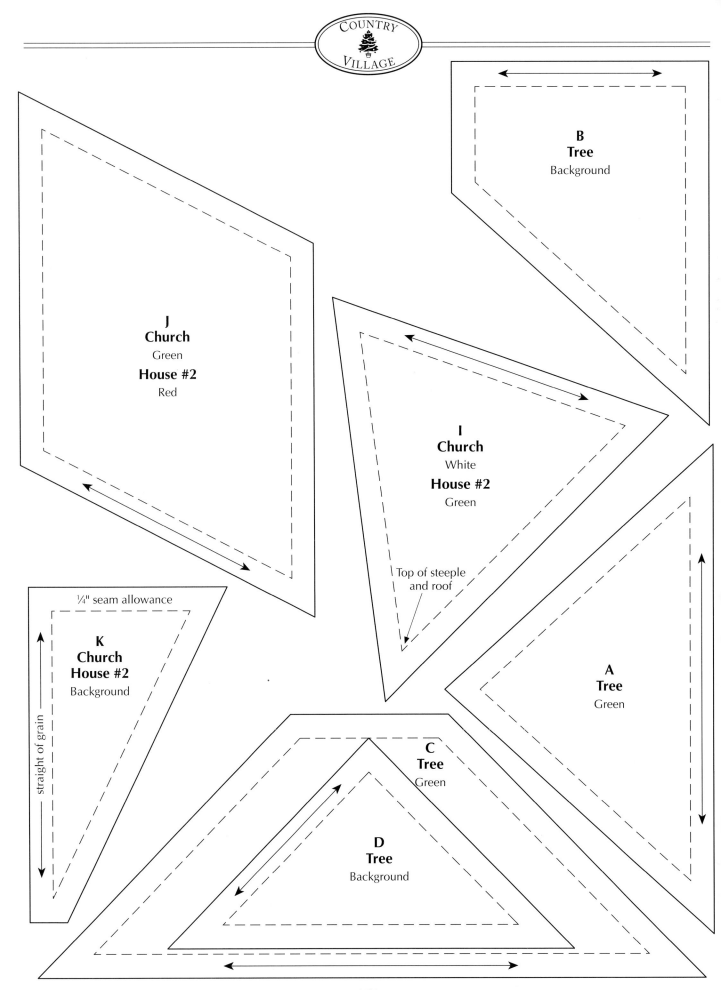

B
Tree
Background

J
Church
Green
House #2
Red

I
Church
White
House #2
Green

Top of steeple
and roof

¼" seam allowance

K
Church
House #2
Background

straight of grain

A
Tree
Green

C
Tree
Green

D
Tree
Background

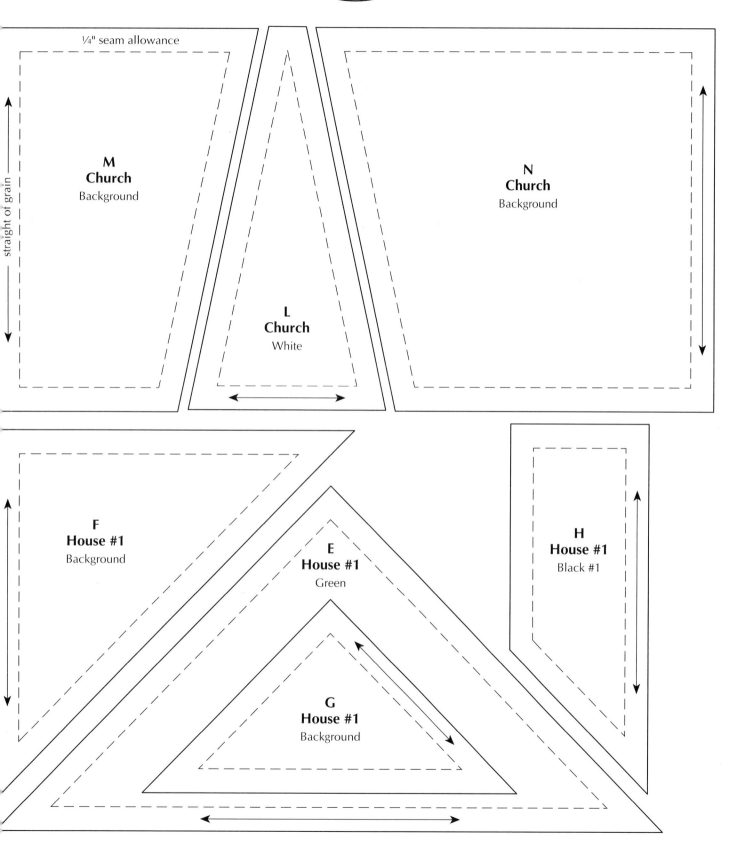

¼" seam allowance

straight of grain

M
Church
Background

N
Church
Background

L
Church
White

F
House #1
Background

E
House #1
Green

G
House #1
Background

H
House #1
Black #1

Dreaming of a
White Christmas

by Joan Gaestel Macfarlane

◄ Delicate tulle angels, pearl garlands, and embellished glass ornaments frost this lovely tree befitting a Christmas bride.

The tree skirt is an extravagant mantle of white satin and pearls. ▶

Dreamy white satin stockings are embellished with pearl beading. The mantel garland is twined with ribbons, pearls, and tiny bouquets of winter-white flowers. (Lower right)

A beaded white satin star, topped off with an oversized tulle bow, crowns this elegant tree. ▼

*E*choing the beauty and tranquillity of Christmas snow and the pure elegance of bridal attire, the theme for this tree and its accessories is a study in white. Differences in texture and light are achieved with shimmering satin and pearls, used in a variety of ways on the ornaments, garland, skirt, topper, and stockings, and on the wispy tulle ornaments and angels. The ornaments and garland are no-sew and very easy to make, using old-fashioned glass ornaments and notions found in the bridal section of craft and sewing stores. What a perfect tree for an at-home holiday wedding!

To complete this "wedding cake" of a tree as shown in the photos, add ornaments and bows to fill in the spaces and create dimension. Lots of pearl and crystal garlands are the frosting on the cake, and glass grape clusters and crystal snowflakes add more sparkle. Pearl sprays and a large tulle bow add dimension to the star topper. Make large bows from wire-edged ribbon to lay in the tree, then shape and drape the streamers across the branches. Decorate the mantel greenery with the Beaded and Beribboned Garland, adding pale roses and candles. Masses of white poinsettias are the finishing touch. If your living room will be the site of a holiday wedding reception, customize the floral and candle accents to match wedding-party colors.

Trim-the-Tree Shopping List

✔ *White mini lights*
✔ *Wide white wire-edged ribbon for bows*
✔ *White-and-silver sparkle tulle for star-topper trim*
✔ *White pearl sprays*
✔ *Iridescent bead garlands*
✔ *Iridescent glass grape bunches*
✔ *Crystal snowflake ornaments*
✔ *Garland for fireplace mantel*
✔ *Fresh or artificial roses*
✔ *White candles*
✔ *White poinsettias*

JOAN GAESTEL MACFARLANE

Joan Gaestel Macfarlane is co-author of *The Happiest Birthdays* and *The No-Sew Costume Book*, (Viking/Penguin) and of *Parties for Kids* (Publications International, Ltd.). She has also written for national magazines and a local newspaper. When Joan is not busy with her creative endeavors and as the mother of two school-age children, she keeps au courant with the younger generation, teaching three-year-olds in nursery school. Joan has been dabbling with creative media of all kinds since she was a young girl and has no intention of stopping anytime soon!

Beaded and Beribboned Garland

Finished Size: 15" loop

Interlocking loops of ribbon and beads, swept together with a beribboned cluster of floral sprays, drape the mantel in style. Because of its interlocking design, the garland can be made in a variety of lengths to accommodate any mantel, wreath, or doorway arch. Just make additional 15" loops!

Materials for each 15" loop

1⅓ yds. of ¼"- or ⅜"-wide white double-faced satin ribbon
1⅓ yds. of prestrung iridescent beads
4 stems of white star-flower clusters or pearl sprays
1 stem of white floral sprays

Assembly

1. Fold the ribbon in half and finger-press center fold.
2. Lay the ribbon and bead strand together on a flat surface; treat them as one while making the garland.
3. Fold each end of the ribbon and bead strand into the center of the ribbon to form a bow shape with 5"- to 6"-long streamers.

4. Secure bow shape with the 5 floral stems grouped together. To do this, position the stems over the center of the bow, with the flowers extending below, then wrap the stems around the bow center until no stem ends remain free.

5. Place the bead streamers only at the center of the bow, overlapping slightly, to form 2 loops. To secure loops in place, make a small, tight bow with the remaining ribbon streamers.

Tie ribbon streamers into bow to secure bead streamer loops in place.

6. To interlock the next garland loop, slip one end of the next ribbon/bead strand through either end of the completed garland loop. Continue from step 3 to the finish, adding as many loops as required.

Star Topper

Finished Size: 7" x 11"

Pearl garlands and iridescent beads dress up a softly sculptured star. Pearl-accented garlands come in a variety of designs and are inexpensive but eye-catching. They generally come packaged in 10-foot lengths and are sold wherever Christmas decorations are available. Strung pearls and sequins are suitable options. Perch the star on the uppermost branch of the tree, then accent with a large tulle bow and pearl sprigs. It will take about 1 yard of 8"-wide tulle for the bow.

Materials

⅜ yd. of 45"-wide lightweight, white satinlike fabric (Look for one with an iridescent shimmer.)
12" x 12" piece of polyester batting
1½ yds. of pearlized bead and star garland
⅓ yd. of prestrung crystal beads
6" length of pearl garland with ¼"-diameter pearls
6" piece of ¼"-wide double-faced satin ribbon
White thread

Cutting

Use pattern on pullout pattern sheet #2.
1. Trace the pattern onto plain paper and cut out.
2. Fold the satin in half lengthwise and cut 2 stars.
3. Cut 1 star from polyester batting.

Assembly

1. Place 1 fabric star, right side down, and place the batting star on top, aligning the edges. Baste fabric and batting together ¼" from the raw edges.
2. Pin remaining star to the star with batting, right sides together, with raw edges even.
3. Stitch ½" from the raw edges, leaving a 2" opening for turning along the edge of one of the bottom points.

Leave open for turning.

4. Trim threads and be sure batting is free of loose threads and debris that could show through the white fabric once it is turned right side out.
5. Carefully turn the star right side out. Gently finger-press the star edges.
6. Invisibly hand stitch the opening closed.
7. Secure star/bead garland along the edges of the star, invisibly hand-tacking approximately ½" or so.
8. Position the pearl garland at the lower center of the star, forming a horseshoe shape; hand-tack in place.
9. Position the remaining bead strand on the star so the beads begin in the lower left star point, move up and around the horseshoe, and then come down to the lower right star point. Hand-tack in place.
10. Position the ribbon ends on the center back of the star to form a loop for securing the star to the tree. Hand stitch in place.

Pearlized Tree Skirt

Finished Size: 44" diameter

Pearl-accented tree garlands border a shimmering skirt. Like the star above it, the skirt is softly sculptured and has a luxurious look.

Materials

1⅓ yds. of 45"-wide lightweight, white satinlike fabric to match star
1⅓ yds. of 45"-wide lightweight white lining
⅔ yd. of polyester batting
4 yds. of pearlized bead and star garland
3¼ yds. of pearl garland with ¼"-diameter pearls
1¾ yds. of ¼"- or ⅜"-wide white double-faced satin ribbon
White thread

Cutting

1. Enlarge the skirt pattern onto tissue paper or pattern tracing cloth and cut out.

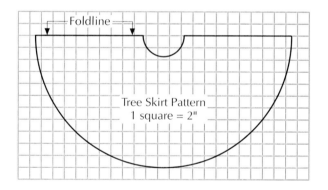

Foldline

Tree Skirt Pattern
1 square = 2"

2. Fold the satin in half crosswise. Pin the pattern to the fabric with the fold line even with fabric fold. Cut 1 skirt piece. Repeat with batting and lining.

Assembly

1. Place the skirt lining, right side down, and lay the batting on top of it, aligning the raw edges. Machine baste ¼" from the edges. Hand baste through both layers from the bottom edge to the inner edge, spacing rows 4" apart. This will keep the layers from shifting while you work.
2. Pin the satin skirt to the lining with right sides together and raw edges even.
3. Stitch ½" from the raw edges, leaving a 6"-long opening for turning.
4. Trim threads and make sure the batting is free of loose threads or debris that could show through the white fabric once it's turned.
5. Carefully turn the skirt right side out. Gently finger-press the edges.
6. Invisibly hand stitch the opening closed.
7. Starting at an open edge, place the garland of large pearls along the lower edge in a wave pattern approximately 2" high and 1" from the bottom edge. Continue the wave pattern all the way around the skirt edge to the other opening edge, pinning as needed.
8. Invisibly hand stitch the garland in place every inch or so to secure it.
9. Starting near an open edge, place the other garland on the skirt in a slightly wavy pattern, approximately 2" from the crest of the garland wave below. Continue around the skirt to the other open edge, pinning as you work.

White-10

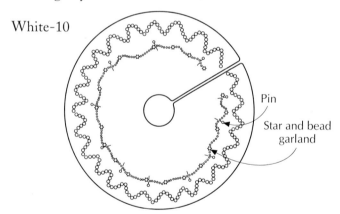

Pin

Star and bead garland

10. Invisibly hand stitch the garland in place to secure.
11. Find the center of the skirt along the top edge and locate the center of the white satin ribbon. Working on the right side of the skirt, align the center of the ribbon with the center of the skirt and the top edge of the ribbon with the top edge of the skirt; pin. Stitch the ribbon to the skirt along the top and bottom ribbon edges.

Center

Veiled Ornament

Finished Size: 3" diameter

Fine-mesh netting, star-flower clusters, and satin ribbon adorn a glossy glass ball for another variation on the elegant white-on-white look. Although tulle netting is available in standard fabric widths, it is also sold on a spool in a 6" width, which is ideal for ornament making.

Materials for 1 ornament

3"-diameter white glass-ball ornament with crown
¾ yd. of 6"-wide fine white tulle
4 stems of white star-flower clusters or other flower and pearl spray of your choice
⅝ yd. of ¼"- or ⅜"-wide double-faced satin ribbon, cut in half

Assembly

1. Fold tulle in half crosswise. Cut on the fold, forming 2 pieces.
2. Slide both tulle pieces halfway through the hoop on the crown of the ornament.
3. Drape the tulle over the ornament, veiling it completely. Gather the tulle at the base of the ornament with your fingers and secure it by wrapping one of the star flowers around, halfway up the stem, and twisting it together.
4. Add the remaining star-flower stems.
5. Sculpt the flowers and stem ends with your fingers over the spray of tulle formed by the gathering.
6. Tie 1 piece of ribbon around the gathers, allowing streamers to fall freely. Slip the remaining ribbon piece halfway through the crown hoop and tie ends together, approximately 1" down, to form a loop for hanging. (See illustration above.)

Ethereal Angels

Finished Size: 4"–5" tall

Embroidered or plain organdy leaves turn a simple piece of folded tulle into something heavenly. Two different sizes of angels are featured here with single- and double-wing options. You can cut the tulle straight across, slightly on the diagonal, or in a jagged fashion to vary the angelic look. They're so easy, fast, and fun to make that you'll have a collection of angels before you know it!

Materials for 1 Angel

8" or 10" piece of 6"-wide fine white tulle
2 plain 3½" organdy leaves or 2" embroidered leaves

Assembly

1. Fold the tulle in half crosswise. Gather the tulle together with your fingers, approximately ½"–¾" from the fold, to form the angel's head.
2. Place the bottom edge of 1 leaf along the gathered area, then twist the stem around until only ½" of the stem remains, securing the head and creating a wing.

3. Secure the second leaf/wing as you did the first, placing the bottoms of the leaves together. Sculpt the leaves with your fingers, if necessary, to look like wings. To create a double-winged angel, simply secure another pair of leaves as you did the first, positioning them slightly lower than the first
4. Twist the remaining stem ends slightly together to form a halo (circle). Hang by the halo or add an ornament hanger or tiny loop of narrow white ribbon to the halo for hanging.

Cascading Pearls Ornament

Finished Size: 3" diameter

Sprays of pearl beads and flowers and satin-backed ribbon transform old or new glass balls into stunning tree ornaments with a vintage look. If purchasing new ornaments, look for balls with a glossy or satin finish (to reflect the decorations and lights) and with crowns (tops) that have holes in them, which allow you to add the decorations easily.

Materials for 1 ornament

3"-diameter white glass-ball ornament with crown
3 stems of white pearl clusters
2 stems of white pearl sprays
3 stems of white floral sprays
⅓ yd. of ¼"- or ⅜"-wide double-faced satin ribbon

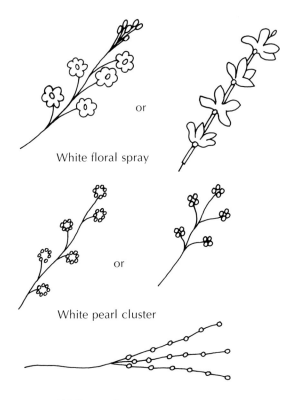

White floral spray

or

White pearl cluster

or

White pearl spray

Assembly

1. One at a time and in consecutive order, carefully slide the stems of the pearl clusters and floral sprays through the holes at the top of the ornament crown, leaving enough of each stem showing so the decorative section begins ½" from the crown.

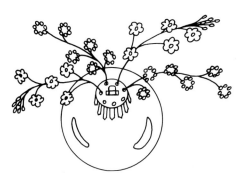

2. Slide pearl spray stems through any remaining holes or through the center crown opening.
3. Finger-sculpt the stems and decorations so they gently cascade over the ornament.
4. Slide the ribbon halfway through the hoop in the crown. Tie the ends together, about 1" down, to form a loop for hanging.

Tip: To secure decorations on ornaments that do not have holes in the crowns, carefully remove the crown, put the stems through the opening as described above, then carefully replace the crown. Continue as above.

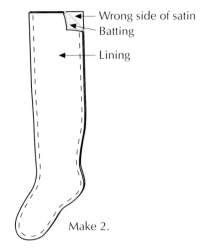

Wrong side of satin
Batting
Lining

Make 2.

Pearlized Stockings
Finished Size: Approximately 11" x 25"

Iridescent prestrung beads and a starry garland on a simply shaped, softly sculptured stocking complete the look of this Christmas theme.

Materials for 2 stockings

1 yd. of 45"-wide lightweight white satinlike fabric to match tree skirt and star
1 yd. of 45"-wide lightweight white lining
1 yd. of polyester batting
2/3 yd. of prestrung iridescent beads
1/2 yd. of star-and-bead garland
5"-long piece of white satin ribbon
White thread

Cutting

Use pattern on pullout pattern sheet #3.
1. Trace the stocking pattern onto tissue paper or pattern tracing cloth and cut out.
2. Fold the satin fabric in half lengthwise and cut 2 pieces for each stocking. Repeat with the lining. Cut 1 piece of batting for each stocking.

Assembly

1. Place 1 stocking piece, right side down, and lay the batting on top of it, raw edges even; pin and machine baste together 1/4" from the edges.
2. Place the batting/stocking, batting side up, and lay the lining on top of it, wrong side down, with raw edges even. See illustration above right. Pin and baste 1/4" from edges. Make 2.
3. Pin and stitch a satin stocking to each satin/batting/lining stocking with right sides together, using a 1/2"-wide seam allowance and leaving the top edge open. Turn right side out.
4. Measure down 9" from the top of the stocking and pin-mark; turn stocking top to the inside, folding along the 9" mark. Hand-tack the inside edge in place.
5. Turn the folded edge down to form a 4½"-deep cuff.

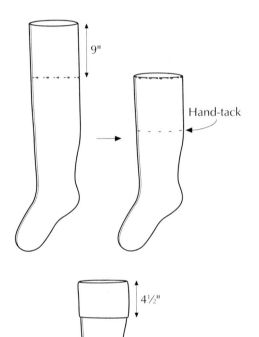

9"

Hand-tack

4½"

6. Place prestrung beads in a wave pattern, approximately 1" high and ½" from the bottom edge of the cuff, starting and ending at the seam. See the photo on page 153. Invisibly hand stitch the garland in place.
7. Position star and bead garland in a slightly wavy pattern just a bit above the bead waves, beginning and ending at the seam; pin and invisibly hand stitch in place to secure.
8. To finish off the stocking, place ribbon ends together, forming a loop. Position it just inside the stocking along the seam edge; hand stitch to secure.